THE HOOKED RUG

HOOKED CARPET AMERICAN EIGHTEENTH CENTURY

Varied close hooking of fine type, with the flowers modeled in rare relief. Resonant black field with banded pink and gray oblong center occupied by diamond medallion having oval leaf scrolled center, enriched with golden lyre motives; surrounded by sprays and corner baskets of lovely modeled pastel colored flowers. Broad finely balanced border developing on the inner edge and center vines of pink and lavender berries; on the outer edge scrolling vines and corners of old pink flowers. Finished with bandings of blue, red and tan stripes. The great difficulties to be overcome after procuring the very beautiful design for this superb piece of American craftsmanship were many. In the first place no loom was in existence to weave the foundation burlap in one piece, viz. 14 by 15 *feet* and consequently a handloom had to be set up to weave the foundation. It is said that forty women were engaged on this work of love and patience and that it was eventually presented to a " Public Athenaeum " in Boston. It is in remarkably fine condition, the pile is still over half an inch thick and with sturdiness of hooking will survive undoubtedly another hundred years.

Size: 14 feet 8 inches x 13 feet 7 inches

THE HOOKED RUG

A Record of Its Ancient Origin · Modern Development · Methods of Making · Sources of Design · Value as a Handicraft · The Growth of Collections · Probable Future in America · And Other Data

BY

WILLIAM WINTHROP KENT

Member of American Institute of Architects, Architectural
League of New York

Foreword by
WILL H. LOW, N.A.

*With more than
one hundred and seventy-five illustrations*

TUDOR PUBLISHING COMPANY

NEW YORK - 1941

Republished by Tower Books, Book Tower, Detroit, 1971

Library of Congress Catalog Card Number 78-172437

TO THOSE

WHO WERE THE FIRST TO RENEW THE EARLY APPRECIATION AND
ENCOURAGE THE REVIVAL IN AMERICA OF RUG HOOKING, PROMINENT
AMONG WHOM ARE:

> MRS. HELEN R. ALBEE OF PEQUAKET, N. H.
> MR. AND MRS. DOUGLAS VOLK OF NEW YORK.
> MR. R. W. BURNHAM, IPSWICH, MASS.
> MR. E. C. HOWE, BOSTON, MASS.
> MR. JAMES A. KEILLOR OF B. ALTMAN & CO.
> MRS. ALICE VAN LEER CARRICK, BOSTON.
> MR. JAMES M. SHOEMAKER, NEW YORK.
> MISS ELIZABETH H. ROWE OF NEW YORK.
> MR. C. E. LAWRENCE, BELMONT, MASS.
> MR. J. W. T. WETTLESON, RUTLAND, VERMONT.
> MRS. ELIZABETH LOUNSBERY.

AND THE MANY COLLECTORS, WHO HAVE NOT ONLY DERIVED FROM
THE STUDY OF HOOKED RUGS, GREAT PLEASURE, BUT ALSO PRESERVED
VALUABLE SPECIMENS OF A PRE-HISTORIC HANDICRAFT, THIS AT-
TEMPT IS DEDICATED.

FOREWORD

WHEN my good friend and neighbor Mr. William Winthrop Kent, first proposed to me that I should write a foreword for his monograph on ' Hooked Rugs ' there was a natural hesitation on my part as my knowledge of his subject was so limited.

But if this limitation applied to the subject of his book, I could say with truth that my acquaintance with its author went back many years to a time when the late George B. Post was President of the Architectural League of New York, and in his absence the writer, as Vice-President, fractionally occupied his chair and presided at one of its dinners. A competition for the cover design of the catalogue for its annual exhibition had just been concluded, and the pleasant duty devolved upon the Vice-President of awarding the prize to Mr. Kent, who among the many competitors — all trained architects — had won it by the merit of his design.

This was only the beginning — Emerson says somewhere that we are a land of beginnings — for, some years afterwards I found myself a neighbor of the laureate, at Lawrence Park, Bronxville, and with the resulting ampler acquaintance has come the conviction that Mr. Kent is among the few in this land of ours who have deliberately stood aside from its engrossing material preoccupations to study and make his own the knowledge of all phases of art from its lightest manifestations to its humblest expression.

This is not the place to speak of Mr. Kent's work for many years as a practicing architect: the buildings exist and can speak for themselves, nor of the many scholarly articles in technical journals due to his cultivated pen, nor even of his more important study of the life and work of Baldassare Peruzzi, architect and painter of the fifteenth century, which adds much to our knowledge of this gifted artist, beyond the meager outline furnished by Vasari.

Undoubtedly it is a far call from studies like these to this monograph on the hooked rug; which has hardly the pretension of an art, but is more of a craft. But ' the saving grace of art ' lurks often in unsuspected places, and we may well be grateful that we have a student in the author of this work to whom no research is insignificant when his keen appreciation once detects a sign of this ' saving grace.'

Virtually alone among the nations we have in our brief history, and by the very circumstances of our growth, little or no art of the people; that peasant art which in the countries of the old world has furnished in many instances the seed from which the greater expressions of art have grown. All the more important is it that what little we have of this precious eclosion of the art spirit should be studied and preserved. In our early days on the shores of this continent, we were children of the Reformation, to whom all art was abhorrent as a legacy from the form of religion from which these early settlers had revolted. But, at the same time, amidst the hard conditions, the penury and distress imposed by the first necessity of gaining a foothold upon an inhospitable shore, there was an isolated housewife, who from the primary necessity of keeping her feet warm, wove into the fabric of her rug some trace of beauty, a simple flower, or the unconscious charm of a pattern. It is surely well that we, later and more sophisticated artists, should recognize and cherish these humble beginnings, and where, through practice and self-education, these unconscious artists perchance did a work that rose in scale to be worthy of comparison with more savant and consciously ambitious weaves, should honor them.

The author makes clear that the hooked rug had its origin in re-

FOREWORD

mote antiquity and probably amid Scandinavian influences, but its chief production seems to have been in this country and at a comparatively late date. This is an additional reason why we should esteem the painstaking research and the critical yet enthusiastic appreciation of a scholar like Mr. Kent, for as already said, our country is notably poor in manifestations of the art spirit and of students capable of rescuing from oblivion their few productions.

WILL H. LOW, N. A.

INTRODUCTION

A NY HANDICRAFT, whatever its source, which endures through
the ages, and interests and occupies thousands of workers, artists
and collectors deserves more than casual attention.

The revived appreciation of all primitive, and especially of early
American, art has brought with it great and increasing interest in
Hooked Rugs. They appeal not only to discerning collectors, but to
textile designers and especially to the public who care for such things.
Yet in spite of this, there so far has not yet appeared in magazine article
or book any full, searching and historical discussion of the probable
origin of this handicraft, excellent as these are in general nor perhaps is
this following account complete. It can be carried further by some
one, I hope.

These are a few reasons for this writing, others being the great possibilities in the development, along peculiar lines of design, of rugs of
this kind, and the fact that their making will probably always be a pure
handicraft, of which the economic value is so great as to have received
the attention of the United States Government.

The valuable help received as to origin, process, the gift of plates,
materials, photographs, etc., from Mr. James A. Keillor of Messrs. B.
Altman & Co.; from Messrs. Lord & Taylor, Messrs. Halle Bros., Cleve-
land; Messrs. Flint & Kent, Buffalo; John Wanamaker; Mr. R. W.
Burnham, Ipswich, Mass.; Mr. Frederick Eccles, Mr. Homer Eaton
Keyes, Editor of *Antiques;* and the inspiration and encouragement de-
rived from Miss Elizabeth H. Rowe's New York collection; from Mrs.
Helen R. Albee's ' Abnakee Rugs '; Miss Amy Mali Hicks' ' The

[xi]

Craft of Handmade Rugs '; from the various books and magazine articles and collections respectively of Miss Frances L. Sutherland, Mrs. Elizabeth Lounsbery, Miss Alice Van Leer Carrick, Mrs. A. L. M. Phillips' book, ' Hooked Rugs and How to Make Them ', Mrs. Elizabeth Waugh's book, ' Collecting Hooked Rugs'; from Mr. A. F. Kendrick of the Textile Department, South Kensington Museum; Messrs. B. T. Batsford, London, England; and Mr. Ernest Marchetti, head of John Crosby & Sons, Ltd., Halifax, England; Mr. R. A. Mackenzie, Leeds, England; Mrs. E. O. Schernikow, New York; Mr. Caswell Barrie, Scarsdale, N. Y.; Mr. & Mrs. Stephen Van Rensselaer; Mr. Wm. Monell, also the Bureau of Fashion & Decoration, of Lord & Taylor's; Mrs. Richard A. Lindabury; Messrs. Paton and Baldwin, Halifax, England; Mr. & Mrs. E. C. Gude, White Plains, N. Y.; James M. Shoemaker Co., New York; *Country Life in America;* Mrs. Frey Broberg, Staten Island, N. Y.; Mr. & Mrs. John C. Spring of Boston, Mass.; Messrs. Clifford & Lawton of *The Upholsterer,* New York; *The Decorative Furnisher,* New York; *The Amer. Carpet & Upholstery Journal,* New York; Mr. Mitchell Kennerley of the Anderson Galleries, New York City; Mr. J. B. Moffat, Bronxville, N. Y., and especially from Miss Ann Macbeth of Penrith, Cumberland, England, Art Instructor at the University of Glasgow, Scotland; Mr. Charles Hanson Towne of *Harpers Bazar;* the *Antiquarian Mag.,* New York; H. W. Frohne, *Good Furniture Magazine,* Grand Rapids, and many others is most gratefully acknowledged herewith.

WILLIAM WINTHROP KENT

Bronxville, N. Y.
January, 1930.

[xii]

CONTENTS

THE HOOKED RUG

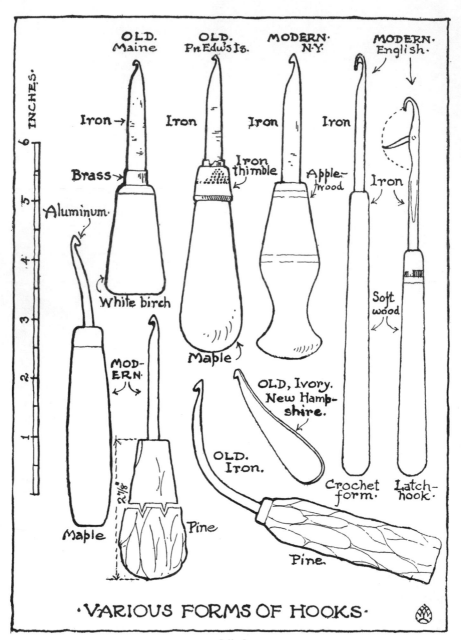

·VARIOUS FORMS OF HOOKS·

CHAPTER I

The First Traces Found of Possible Origin Abroad

THE HOOKED RUG is a fascinating subject for discussion. Of lowly origin, its earliest designs are often beautiful in pattern and color; an art practiced originally by prehistoric workers for clothing and later by poor people from necessity, carried on, from the savings of domestic rag bags, to give warmth to the bed and decency and cheer to the bare floor of the cottage, it spread from house to house, from farm to farm, from village to village in many lands; gradually these rugs found a place in the home of the well-to-do in many a town, and after an apparent lapse into what seemed oblivion for years, its early and late products have to-day in America been eagerly collected and have even forced down the price of oriental rugs, upsetting somewhat the market therefor. They have been gathered eagerly into the mansion of many a wealthy connoisseur in Europe and America among his most cherished possessions. Truly a remarkable history and one worthy of more scholarly research and careful study than has yet been given it or than the present writer is able now to give, even after years of work thereupon.

The charm which so many find in rugs comes partly from the good color and pattern composition. But there is a more indefinable quality, the personality of the maker so often in them. This is well illustrated by the following extract from a letter from Tennessee to the *Rural New Yorker,* a periodical which is hailed with delight by farm dwellers for its clean and helpful news, instructive counsel and brave defense of the agriculturist. A Mrs. D. B. P. wrote to it not long ago, anent hooked rugs:

'I enjoy making my own designs. I never knew how to sing or paint or draw; no way to express myself, only by *hoeing,* washing, ironing, patching, etc., and while I never hope to accomplish anything extraordinary, I do love to plan out and execute *these rugs that are a bit*

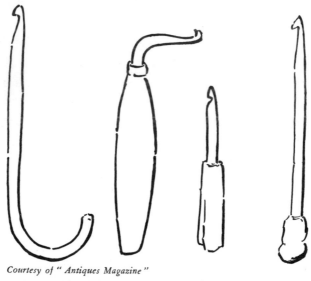

Courtesy of " Antiques Magazine "

OTHER FORMS OF HOOKS [#1a]

of myself, a blind groping after something beautiful (italics added). But when one is finished, it is a disappointment, the colors don't blend, or some are too glaring, *but one keeps on trying.'*

It does not lessen the romantic quality of the tale, that in the great flock of designs from this art there are many ugly ducklings. It could not be otherwise when so many untutored minds and hands have had to do with it, nor is that fact of special significance or interest. Crude indeed are the efforts of many of the thousands of tireless workers, in farm and hamlet here and abroad, but lovely are the works of the most gifted ones, indeed we may call some American specimens superb, for

they are not only beautiful, but new and original contributions to the art of the world, that reveal often the personality of the maker in their pattern and their color arrangement. It may be too that this vigorous personality in the best specimens is what has so attracted the American public and is even now attracting foreigners in England and on the continent.

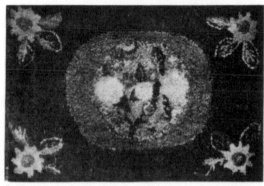

Courtesy of " The Rural New Yorker"

Modern unsheared woollen rug made in Tennessee, by Mrs. D. B. P. [#2]

Some people, rightly or wrongly, are tired of the average modern oriental rug in which

Now in Collection of Mr. and Mrs. Charles Billings Gleason, Cleveland, Ohio

Early American, clipped wool, found in Topsfield, Maine. Ivory field, bright red flowers, pink buds, brown basket, " hit-or-miss " brilliant border. Probably made by a Mrs. Landers, a French Canadian, of distinguished character. She was 92 years old and a delightful personality. [#3]

patterns of great historic value have been through the years so often ignorantly translated into meaningless shapes and colors by successive generations of untaught and weary workers, that now the significance of pattern and color has been almost lost. They do not always speak clearly to us, because they have so little to say, unless we chance upon a good antique oriental rug of pro-

[3]

hibitive price, whereas the average hooked rug of considerable beauty, and still within the means of the average citizen, can distinctly say a great deal.

With the loss of historic significance in the oriental rug has gone also to a great extent the knowledge of color building and pattern

Very early American (or English) rug in the collection of Oliver Williams Esq. at Witch or Garrison House, Rockport, Mass. Note the distorted scroll forms originally suggested by carvings on Tudor furniture. [#4]

scheme. The really *old* oriental rugs show deep artistic feeling and inspired knowledge. It was not enough for their designers that a rug should merely contain complementary colors with hackneyed patterns, but themes of tone and harmony and great richness were sought and attained by the most inspired workers, in gradation or building up of color in changing tones, until the best effect that the artist could secure was obtained. The pattern was studied in its relation to the color scheme and *vice versa,* and if this art was all, or much of it, imitative, it nevertheless in ancient days revealed the mind and hand of the author.

Perhaps too the fact that the modern American student of decoration finds the modern oriental rug a hard thing to combine with the furniture and mural tones of the colonial or other simple interior has had much to do with the fall of that rug from favor, but however the change has come, the fact remains that the hooked rug has won thousands of devotees while some other rugs have lost admirers.

[4]

You can date the great revived appreciation of hooked rugs from the time when we began to note the beauty of genuine antique Chinese rugs. There is a quality in good hooked rugs akin to the best old Chinese. In both there is revealed vigor, fresh, fearless thought and enthusiastic searching for the best that can be done. Let us look further into the Orient.

Japan had its color prints or 'ukiyoye' for the man in the street and the toiler of town and farm, but Europe and America had their popular art in the hooked rug. Each is the result of the urge for self-expression through an art and a handicraft which quickly became popular. This longing to say something to fellow men through manual work in color and pattern has often come to many classes of mankind, but while the Japanese

Another rug in the collection of Oliver Williams Esq. at Rockport, Mass. A richly decorative primitive design. [#5]

block color print was made and sold considerably in the Japanese cities, the hooked rug was, although of foreign origin, especially an art and resource of the American farm or the small town, at least in the best period. Both arts were of relative importance to their publics, both have been despised and excessively praised; somewhere between these extremes lies the truth, which in the case of the rug the writer tries to indicate herein.

From the third to the seventh century, A.D., and possibly longer, the Copts, descendants of the ancient Egyptians, made fine, tightly drawn or woven, and also coarser, looser embroidery which was based on the appreciation of the artistic possibilities of loops of colored wool left *standing, above* the surface of a basic material of coarse or of fine cloth. The art was probably ancient even then, and is seen to-day in certain oriental weavings. This process was continued by succeeding generations. It was followed also by later oriental and possibly no-madic weavers, and probably brought into Spain by the Moors, Arabs

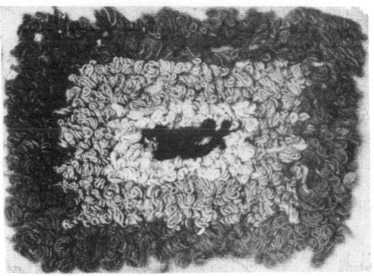

Courtesy of Metropolitan Museum of Art, N. Y.
A COPTIC MAT CIRCA SIXTH CENTURY [#6]

and Berbers, whose descendants, the Moriscos of Las Alpuharras, driven in 1609 into the fastnesses of the south slopes of the Sierra Nevada mountains in Andalusia not far from Granada, obtained in certain hangings and rugs almost this same Coptic character. Their successors continued the art until about one hundred years ago, when the work was apparently abandoned. Probably other peoples em-ployed the same process, with similar results.

In the illustration here given of Coptic work of about the

[6]

Courtesy of "The American Home"

Old French-Canadian hooked runner dyed with home-made dyes. Latter half nineteenth century, unsheared, and evidently a farm product. From "The Magic Dyes of Olden Days," by Douglas Leechman. [#7]

sixth century A.D., the likeness to the effect secured by the rug weavers of Las Alpuharras, Spain, in some of their fabrics, and to that of certain hooked rugs of Europe and America, is striking.

Mrs. John Albee (Helen R. Albee), whose booklet on ' Abnakee Rugs ' (hooked) is well known, learning of the wide search for all possible data on the origin of hooked rugs, kindly drew my attention to certain special Coptic embroideries in the Metropolitan Museum of Art, which had been studied with interest years ago. I had not then, however, found any example suggesting a hooking process. Closer examination of much of the embroidery in the Textile Department there, and especially of the example illustrated, convinced me that there was, however, similarity in effect between the Coptic and the hooking process, and that the Alpuharras rugs were possibly in some way one of the modern links between these ancient Egyptian examples of weaving and our more modern clipped and unclipped hooked rugs. So far I have seen no Coptic work that was clipped or sheared to make an even surface, but the loops appear sometimes to have been drawn by an implement over some form, to secure evenness of height. The best of the early style of modern hooked rugs also show the even, unclipped loops, although excellent rugs, perhaps the best, have also been made clipped. Mrs. Albee writes of a beautiful counterpane which she saw some years ago at St. Simon's Island, which she thinks had been made exactly as the Coptic work was done, but perhaps she is noting the effect rather than the process. This, she believes, is fit to stand beside the Coptic work to show the power of beauty in the perpetuation of a handicraft. Early American rugs are found showing the same effect. All this does not mean that the hooking process sprang directly from Coptic or Spanish work, but only that the old work may have inspired the new, through succeeding ages of rug making. Whether this is true or not the likeness alluded to is very interesting.

[8]

EARLY AMERICAN FLORAL HOOKED RUG

Striated brown field; occupied by jardinière of loose pink and crimson flowers. Triangular corners of mosaic in crimson, blue, ivory and blue-black. [#8]   *Size: 4 feet 6 inches x 3 feet 2 inches.*

Collection of Jas. M. Shoemaker Co., N. Y.   Courtesy of " Antiques Magazine "

Early New England rug of wool and probably on home-woven linen. [#9]

[9]

So much for certain ancient beginnings of certain rug processes and their continuance, as far as determined. The hunt for early traces of the origin of actual *hooked* rug making may be described as follows:

After many years of correspondence with individuals connected with art and industry both in America and Europe certain facts were brought to light which very clearly show that the hooked rug did not originate in America (in which term is included both the United States and Canada), but in Europe and, more exactly where, the words of my correspondents as quoted will show. Tracing the art through these letters in the order received, the most important facts are given last of all.

At the start the subject of their *foreign* origin was approached through friends abroad, museum authorities, merchants and manufacturers and latterly through antiquarians and a teacher of handicraft. From all these sources and talks also with individuals in America came the data set forth for the reader's criticism.

The first credible facts of the European origin of hooking came to the writer only after a long time and considerable research and letter writing. There was no authority known whom one could fruitfully question or refer to, most writers and collectors could only guess and advance ungrounded opinions and this they freely did. To learn facts it was necessary to grope and seize on each and every chance for enlightenment, talk with collectors, rug makers, and where possible with Canadians of the various provinces, and Europeans. This the writer did constantly for several years and while every one approached was willing, no one knew or could help, until the way was opened by foreign correspondence. Even then the progress was slow and the results often meager and baffling. It could not be pushed and it extended through years, often it seemed a foolish or trifling pursuit, a wild goose chase or that some will-o-the-wisp was leading on and on. Did any

EARLY AMERICAN MEDALLION HOOKED RUG

Pale blue oval medallion, occupied by long bouquet of crimson and pink roses and buds. Deep leaf scrollings of mulberry at corners.
Size: 4 feet 5 inches x 2 feet 8 inches. [#10]

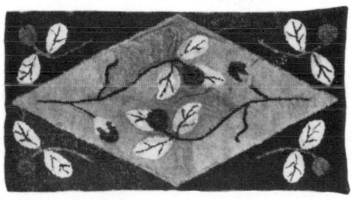

EARLY AMERICAN RAISED MEDALLION HOOKED RUG

Orange-yellow diamond medallion, with sprays of raised crimson-pink flowers. Triangular black corners with sprays of similar flowers.
Size: 4 feet 7 inches x 2 feet 6 inches. [#11]

[11]

one care where hooked rugs came from and would they ever care and what good would it do to know? I think that a love of pattern and color, the knowledge that seafaring folk made these rugs, that many were extremely beautiful, like no other known kinds, that in the process lay great possibilities of development beyond what Americans had yet accomplished, all these things and a certain romance in the quest kept the writer at the game which was played in the sequence which it may be interesting to follow now herein.

Well over one hundred years ago, what is known as hearth rugs were widely used in England; just how much earlier they were first made can hardly be determined now. Many dwellings, especially cottages where no other rug or carpet was used had the hearth rug. Of all men, the Englishman, whatever his lot in life, has always loved his fireside and valued all that embellished it, or added to its comfortable aspect. Hence, among rugs, the hearth rug, from pelt to textile, has in England long held an important place.

In Yorkshire, which, in the nineteenth century, as now, was noted for its weaving industries, as well as in other localities, many weavers in the early days worked in their own cottages, either on their own or a rented loom. In the process of weaving many remnants of woolen yarn were left, in short pieces about 9″ to 18″ long, too short to be of value for further cloth weaving, and these ' thrums,' as they were called, became by custom the property of the weaver, the wool being often supplied by his employer or the man who took the finished cloth and paid for the labor of weaving.

In the opinion of a former Yorkshire weaver with whom I have talked the constant accumulation of these loom ends of woolen yarn logically led to the invention or at least the adoption of some way of utilizing them, other than disposal by sale as rags or waste. What is known as ' brodded ' or pegged rugs had already, he says, been devised

Antique American. Clipped. Obverse or top.
R. W. Burnham Collection. [#12]

Reverse of same showing the basic material and
distinct hooking or "drawing-in." [#13]

A VERY OLD RUG

somewhere earlier than this to utilize the small pieces of cloth, or loom and household remnants, and 'brodded' rugs had already for some years been in use as hearth rugs. The process of 'brodding' was as follows: a skewerlike instrument of metal or hard substance, possibly horn or bone, with a pointed end was thrust down through a piece of cloth or burlap and fairly close to the resulting hole another hole was made in the same way. Then the end of a piece of cloth cut into a narrow strip was *pushed* down through one hole and then through the second one, and more holes made and so threaded, or punched through and the two ends of each piece left standing up an inch or less. When a number of these pieces had been inserted, the ends were clipped off with scissors at a desired height to secure a fairly level surface on the rug. What we now know as 'punched' rug making, as described by Miss Sutherland in 'House Beautiful,' is practically the process of 'brodding.' This utilization of cloth scraps by the 'brodded' rug perhaps led in some part of the world, by logical steps, to the adoption of a process for the utilization of the yarn 'thrums.' This new kind of rug was produced by simply giving the 'brod' or bodkin a hooked end which was similar to the hook form used by very early men, and by which the 'thrum' was *pulled* up through and left standing in a loop. Cloth remnants were also cut into narrow strips and used in the same way as the 'thrums.' These loops of yarn or cloth strips could either be made short and so left close to the basic fabric, or long and then clipped off at the height or varying heights required for certain effects. This is what is done in hooked rug making to-day and has been done for many years, both in Europe and America. But what suggested the hook? This surely was merely a necessary recourse to the very ancient tambour-needle or hook used by women so constantly during the middle ages, to pull threads through cloth tightly stretched on a tambour frame of two hoops one inside the other.

Early American, possibly Canadian. Dark field and ivory wheels with deep red background between the spokes, etc. Collection of Mrs. Charles W. Halsey. [#14]

Courtesy of Mrs. Hayden Richardson

Very old and beautiful rug at The Sign of the Motor Car, Dennis, Cape Cod. Ivory field, dark brown vase, grapes lavender, red and purple, grape leaves and stems dark green, pale flowers near vase, pale blue outline. Big flowers, on vase top, orange with red outline, bell flowers at right pale blue, tulip forms in upper center green and red striped, bell flowers to left of them red and yellow, flower to extreme right red, and blue outline. [#15]

The word ' thrum,' we might note here, is most interesting old English. It is used by many early writers, and is derived from the German ' trum,' a short thick piece, a stump or *end*. To thrum means to stick short pieces of yarn *through,* to twist or knot. Shakespeare says in the ' Merry Wives of Windsor ' (IV:2:80), " There's her thrummed hat," etc., meaning a hat made of weaver's tufts or thrums. It was also spelled ' thrumb.' Barrie uses it in the title ' A Window in Thrums,' as his name for the town of Kerriemuir; Hakluyt speaks of Persian carpets of ' thrummed wool,' and witches were credited with wearing thrum caps of waste yarn, all of which shows its antiquity. (See in general *Century Dictionary.*) But most interesting of all in connection with this subject is the fact that ' thrum mats ' were made anciently by sailors, no one knows how long ago, out of canvas with short strands of yarn or rope put or pulled through it. These were used to place in a ship's rigging, where by their rough surfaces they took up the chafing of ropes. Mr. Hamilton Easter Field in ' The Arts Magazine ' for May, 1921, wrote of a rug in his collection, and executed by a Captain Talpey of the War of 1812. This is made of yarn on sailcloth and is probably like a ' thrum ' mat in technique. It is likely that he was familiar with the art from making similar mats in his youth at sea. The writer personally knows a sailor who now makes many hooked rugs while off duty from a life-saving station, on Cape Cod. Most of these are of cotton strips which he dyes, and are clipped to make a very fluffy mat, and old sailors along shore in many a port, and even inland towns, now make hooked rugs, first cousins to thrum mats.

Thus, it at *first* seemed to the writer that probably by English sailors and weavers a new kind of rug was made, and used and sold too as a hearth rug in Yorkshire, England and Scotland, and that the method of making spread from England throughout northeastern America as more and more colonists came to the new country. There

Very heavy cotton rug of Persian character designed and made by Mrs. Davis, Forest City, N. B. [#16]

Mrs. K. A. Heath collection, Dover Plains, N. Y.

Blue, salmon and purple, 3 *feet* x 3 *feet* 6 *inches,* unsheared wool and cotton. New Brunswick, Canada. [#17]

was, it appeared, strong probability that this was the origin of the hooked rug. Certainly it then seemed perfectly logical, but more was to come.

Mr. Frederic Eccles, my informant, as to part of the above facts, who is a Yorkshire man and weaver, told me that he personally hooked

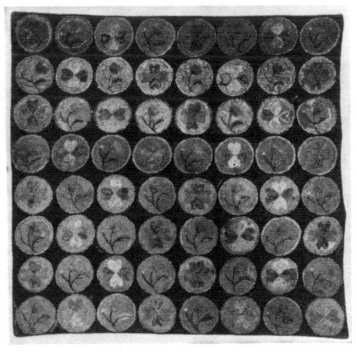

Courtesy Mrs. E. O. Schernikow, N. Y.

The much-sought-for tones of blue predominate in this piece, relieved by ivory, gray, and touches of rose. Circles probably made with a dinner plate. [#18].   *Size: 4 feet 6 inches square.*

rugs in the manner above described, when he was in Yorkshire forty or more years ago, and at that time to his certain knowledge, they had been made for many years previous, and after 'brodded' rugs were

[18]

known. All this of course did not establish that the *first* hooked rug was made in Yorkshire, or even in England or on the seas. We know that constantly invaders, travelers and many weavers came to England from the continent, driven thence by conditions of life in Scandinavia, Germany, France, Holland, etc., earlier than and during the various continental wars and it also seemed possible that the hooked rug for utilizing yarn and cloth remnants was brought by some of these exiles

Courtesy of " Antiques Magazine "

Evidently a homemade design and of farm or village origin. [#19]

and taught to the English weavers. This might well be so, one could argue, as the tambour hooked needle was undoubtedly known on the continent before it was in England. The fact too that hooking is a kind of weaving process and was carried on largely by weavers, at least in its inception, as far as Mr. Eccles could determine from his own observation and experience, pointed to but did not prove its invention by a weaver. It apparently, however, must have been a diverting occupation to all who worked usually at the loom, and deemed a valuable means of utilizing waste yarn.

Right here it is well to note that especially along the seacoasts and the islands hooked rugs are made to-day and have been for many years. This practice of seafaring people pointed to long familiarity with the

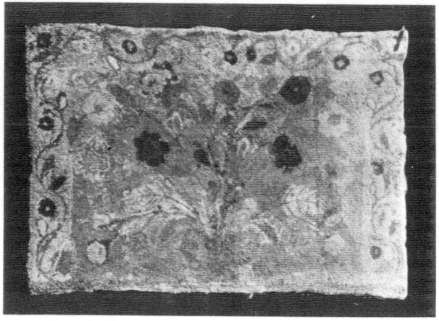

Courtesy of " Antiques Magazine "

According to Gertrude De Wager, the earliest of her Grandmother's mats. Note the absence of black outlines so often wrongly used. A very beautiful rug. [#20]

art (if not to its invention) by sailors — possibly Vikings (see later) — whatever the land of origin.

It is known too that hearth rugs, possibly 'brodded' and possibly the hooked variety which were also known widely as hearth rugs at one time, were sold at least one hundred years ago in Great Britain, for in

the first issue of ' The Manchester Guardian,' May 5, 1821, a certain
W. R. Smalpage, 3 Spring Gardens, Manchester, advertises hearth
rugs for sale at ' 10s. 6d. to 16s.,' along with ' Kidderminster and Venetian ' carpets and ' blankets, druggets and moreens.' Proof of the later
sale of hearth rugs in Scotland also, was given me by Mr. Eccles, who
stated that in his day in Yorkshire, wall-paper designs were used as
suggestions in composing designs for hooked rugs for the hearth and
other places.

Another good reason for believing that the hooking process came
from Europe and did not originate in America was that it was first
noticeably practiced in America in the regions which lie along the northeastern seaboard of this continent, and therefore mostly by English,
Scandinavian, Scotch and many French Canadians. New England and
Canada indeed seem to have been a focus for the art in America, which
was logical in as much as New England and Canada had more English
and Scotch settlers in the earlier days than other parts of America. This
does not overlook the fact that the Canadian French made many beautiful rugs, in fact some of the most beautiful, but I believed at this stage
of my study, that they took up the idea from other colonists some of
whose forebears brought it with them from the old country, although
there was still the possibility it was known in France. So far however,
I have not been able to prove that any hooked rugs were actually made
in France, at any time, but from what I have now learned they were
probably made both long ago and recently in Scotland, and now in
Ireland.

Next came by research the data that many English rugs of half a
century ago were made by the drawn or hooked process, as I was informed by several English authorities and especially by Mr. A. F.
Kendrick, of the Department of Textiles, South Kensington Museum.
These were made chiefly, he stated, by cottagers and sailors and of gray

flannel and red cloth, but not of great artistic value or interest in the main, especially as to pattern, which was perhaps why the purely British product never appealed strongly to later art students or craftsmen.

Courtesy of " Antiques Magazine "

Showing clearly a mosaic effect, in an unclipped rug. [#21]

Other colors used by them were probably all remnants, and the red cloth referred to was the brilliant British army cloth, which in the very early days came from Spain. It was later made in England and prized

[22]

by the North American Indian weavers, notably the Hopis and the Navahoes. They first secured it from Spanish explorers and then from British traders and pioneers and raveled it for use. This fact is most interestingly discussed by Mr. George Wharton James in his excellent book on 'The Navahoe Rug.'

From many letters received next in order from good English authorities on rug making and handicrafts in general, there appeared to be no literature on the making of the hooked rug in England, but in

Courtesy of R. A. Mackenzie, Esq.

Obverse. [#22]   Reverse. [#23]

MODERN ENGLISH PEGGED RUGS
OF WOOLEN
1923, Hope Mills, Leeds, England.

addition to the information given above as to the gray and red cloth being used, Mr. Kendrick also wrote that ' borders of a different color from the middle space, or diamond shapes, are frequently seen and occasionally a *motto* is reproduced.' The latter was probably some form of greeting such as ' Welcome ' or ' Come Again,' as on certain American rugs which are bizarre but not always beautiful although some specimens are delightful in pattern and color.

[23]

After making all the local inquiries about homemade English hooked rugs as far as he was able, Mr. R. A. Mackenzie of Hope Mills, Leeds, England, my next informant who to-day makes the pegged (brodded or prodded) rugs, both by machine and by hand, sent to me in May 1923 specimens of his work which are coarser than the average American hooked rug but done by 'pegging' or 'brodding' on commercial burlap, and made of waste felt and woolen cloth in very coarse strips. He said that hooked rug making as a home industry *to-day* in England is confined to the north i.e. Durham County, and Newcastle-on-Tyne, but the late Mrs. C. W. McAndrew of Headley Park, Borden, Hants, told me she had known of and seen rugs which were recently made in Hants. I now began to believe they are still made in many other English districts, although Mr. Mackenzie wrote at this date that to-day they are 'not known in Yorkshire, the home of the (machine made) rug trade.' He added, 'You would be quite safe in saying the hooked rug has been made in England one hundred years, more than that I wouldn't care to go.' He went on entertainingly to relate, 'I only got to know about a fortnight since what the Hooked Rug is, and strange to say I have two of them in my own house, which I had made at my native town, Elgin, in the north of Scotland, but they are the *first* made up there . . . etc.' In this he may be mistaken.

In another letter of October 22 he stated that 'pegged' or 'prodded' rugs have been made in the Huddersfield and Leeds districts for over one hundred years in the cottage homes, but only within the last twenty years in the factory. 'At home they were made on flat frames in which the canvas was firmly stretched and the clips (or cloth pieces) were pegged through holes made with a steel prodder.'

Often in England sugar bags of coarse linen and burlap were used for a foundation for pegging and for hooking, as was told me by an

Courtesy of " Antiques Magazine "

Evidently New England rugs of wool and of farm or village type. [#24]

Englishman, H. R. Haynes, Esq., of Canton, Mass., who says that when a boy in Lancashire he often saw his mother and grandmother use a wooden peg and a hook to make rugs, and he himself cut cloth into strips for the ' pegging.'

Then it was revealed that to-day they have a simpler method of making this pegged rug in the factory, viz. on an upright frame, with

Collection of Mrs. E. O. Schernikow
EARLY AMERICAN UNSHEARED HOOKED RUG (Circa 1825)
Small mauve vase holds bouquet of flowers in delicate pastel tones of lavender, rose, gray. Branches of similar flowers on either side. Black wool ground.
Size: 44 inches x 27 inches. [#25]

two rollers one above another with cogwheels at right ends thereof. Across the top of the frame is a bar with staples. The canvas, or burlap, is tacked on to the middle roller carried over the staples set ⅝" apart on top bar and then fixed to the bottom roller. Next it is tightened up by the cogwheel action. The cloth clippings after being cut a uniform length are pegged through between the staples of the top bar with a patent needle much like curling tongs in appearance and use.

This product is known in the factory as a ' handmade ' rug, but twenty-five years ago the factory introduced a loom-made, pegged rug finished by a cropping machine which clips the surface evenly. This rug in the Midlands and the north of England displaced the handmade article.

Courtesy of " American Carpet and Upholstery Journal," N. Y.
BEDSIDE HOOKED RUG
Remarkable example of fine hooking on linen. *Size:* 1 *foot* 11 *inches* x 1 *foot* 6½ *inches.* The first specimen here illustrated is a rare example of an early American hooked rug, collected by Mr. and Mrs. James L. Hutchinson on the New England Coast. [#26]

A type found in Northern England to-day. See pages 34, 38, and 40. [#27]

Mr. Ernest Marchetti, the head of John Crossley and Sons L'l'd., Halifax, England, also wrote me on January 14, 1922, through the kindness of Messrs. B. T. Batsford of London, as to the hooked rug that it ' *is still made here in cottage homes (Halifax, England)* . . . and consists of a very loosely woven canvas back, through which threads of yarn are " hooked " and then simply cut off by hand to make a level surface.' He writes also of a rug termed ' Mosaic ' made thereabout some seventy or eighty years ago and that now people *do collect* them,

Courtesy of " Antiques Magazine "
EARLY AMERICAN RAISED MEDALLION HOOKED RUG
Mottled blue-black field, displaying two gray-blue medallions of raised crimson-pink flowers and green leaves. *Size: 3 feet 10 inches x 3 feet.*
[#28]

the price being several pounds, which indicates that they were well made and possibly of considerable beauty. The latter would seem also to be a form of hooked rug common in America now.

Another method of rug making, now practiced in England is revealed by an advertisement. It surely must have come from the prodding or brodding and hooking processes or is at least closely akin to these and to the hooked tambour work. A canvas is used like cross-stitch canvas only coarser, which has every third mesh a large one. It is held on the knee or on a table. The pieces of wool yarn are cut exactly the same length by a gauge. The hook used has a catch or latch on it, (see illustration, ' English,' in plate #1), and is inserted in one hole and out the next in the next row, as follows: The wool is held in the left hand and above the canvas, then doubled and the double end is slipped over the hook, the catch being up or open. The hook is then drawn out through the canvas toward the worker, the cut ends being kept in the left hand. The catch by this action drops down and secures the wool. The tool is next pushed forward through the wool loop and catches the two ends held in the left hand, then the loop is held in the left hand and has the two ends pulled through *it* with the hook. To pull out hook and draw tight the two cut ends finishes the knot. This is really a pile fabric and is known as a Turkey Rug but sprang from the hooking process as the earlier hook used was of the crochet hook form. All the implements for this are on sale at ' The Pattern Shop,' 13 Southampton St. Strand, London W. C. and the wools are made and sold by J. & J. Baldwin, *Halifax, England*. A full account of the process was recently printed in ' Leach's Sixpenny Knitting Series, 23.'

It is indeed strange that there is no literature in England on the hooked rug as made by sailors, cottagers and others, but the fact that the craft was never widely developed there must be the reason for this lack of interest. It would seem worth while even now to take up in England the further study of its beginnings and development at least in conjunction with other and commercial rug making to which it has led. The past neglect of it is strange in a land which has concerned itself wonderfully with the arts and crafts of other countries. Even the superb South Kensington Museum had not a specimen in 1922.

CHAPTER II

The Very Probable Origin Given

FINALLY the most important information so far received which is both the most interesting and conclusive came from Miss Anne Macbeth, Hartsop, Patterdale, Penrith, Cumberland, Great Britain. Miss Macbeth received one of a number of letters broadcast in the mails by the writer in an effort to gain all possible facts. Miss Macbeth is a writer and teacher of handicrafts and of all that is connected with

Courtesy of Mr. and Mrs. John C. Spring, Boston, Mass.

Well designed, colored and worked circular rug, spread on a rounding rock on the lawn. Exquisite example about 6 *feet* in diameter. [#29]

weaving, embroidery, rug and textile making as the reader will infer from her letters; the first is of November 3, 1927, which in the main runs as follows:

'Hooked Rugs are the commonest thing all over what I may term the ancient Kingdom of Strathclyde, which includes the portion of

Britain from North Lanarkshire down to Morecombe Bay, and possibly even further south they are also known as " brodded " rugs.

' Artistically, as a rule, they have little value since they are more often than not made of waste materials and therefore there is little attempt at design. I have another and rather better method of doing them which I will demonstrate if you wish. I have been very much

Courtesy of Jas. M. Shoemaker Co.

Old Basket weave pattern with flower added. [#30]

occupied lately in helping to wake up the various old crafts of these parts and to stimulate them if possible by adjusting them to the conditions of everyday life.

' There was a large quantity of very excellent rugs of the hooked type at an exhibition I judged at Castle Douglas in Galloway only a week or two since and if you wish it I can easily get in touch with the people who did them. In my own Women's Institute in this remote dale of Westmorland we do quite amazingly good work on rugs. Some of the rugs are (now) *woven* with packing needles on a strong warp and are uncommonly good, artistically and from the wearing point of view. One of them quite raised a *furore* in the great Women's Institute Show in London last winter. But this sort is deservedly good since the worker is responsible for both warp and weft and does not work on a canvas already made. We also make rather lovely rugs on a jute matting with handwoven borders done with a needle. . . .

'The "Locker" hooked rug (*as already described*) is done on a large meshed canvas with a hook which has an eyelet on the end into which a thread of thick yarn or string is inserted. The worker then hooks *up* from *beneath* the canvas as many loops as the hook will hold, pulls the thread through the whole lot and the looped pile is then locked *on top* of the canvas and cannot possibly be pulled back again which is the failing of the old fashioned hooking method. . . . They have a fair weight of wool in them — the method is very quick — much quicker than the "hooked" method as usually done. Some of the jute ones I think would " catch on " awfully well in your country. . . . At the moment I have not a single rug in my hands. They are all out travelling the country to help other classes.

'I have for years been chief instructress at the School of Art in Glasgow, trying very hard to get to rock bottom of simplicity in design and technique and independence of working outfit and tools and accessories, so that we can make it possible for everyone to be their own designer and technician. Possibly you might see books on it which I have written, " School and Fireside Crafts " is the main one published by Methuen and Company.'

Here follows in a later letter Miss Macbeth's important historico-traditional account of *whence the process of hooked rug making came to Scotland*:

This waved or agate and stepped pattern was used in many
forms, and is usually beautiful. [#31]

One or two varying forms of this are well-known Maine
and New England patterns, generally excellent. [#31a]

NOVA SCOTIAN PATTERNS

THE HOOKED RUG

(December, 1927 ?)
Hartsop — (Not dated)
Patterdale — Penrith

'Dear Mr. Kent,

'Your letter was sent to Mr. (J. C.) Morland (Glastonbury) by — I think — an antique dealer in Preston, Lancashire (and then to her).

'Now as to history — I fear it is unlikely we can tell you much because these rugs are not held in reverence in this country and no one has troubled to look it up, nor do I think it likely that people will have preserved any old ones, to any great extent.

'But knowing this North Country England as I do and the South of Scotland also — very well, I am quite sure they must have been going from at least *Tudor times*. You can deduce a good deal from the fashion of the houses. All the older ones, till quite recently, had stone-flagged floors and much carven furniture and *the carvings* on the old " bride wains " (which is the local name for the three or four tiered oak cupboards) and on the dressers (which are sideboards with plate racks or locally, " pot rails ") . . . *are all much akin to the more accomplished patterns on the rugs.* The designs as a whole are *not* of a high order and not usually the best, adjusted to the limitation demanded by method of working. The district where I find these rugs indigenous is, roughly speaking, the *Scandinavian Scots* district which was once the Kingdom of Strathclyde and reached from Lanarkshire southwards to Morecombe Bay in Galloway (as before written) and the Stewartry of Kirkcudbright. They really do them (there) best of all I think.

'I see no reason to discredit the theory that they were probably introduced by Scandinavian settlers hereabouts. The names of people and (of) natural features and old household words are strongly Scandinavian and *curiously enough when I lately had the loan of a large volume of reproductions of rugs made in Finland the resemblance was*

[34]

One form of basket-weave pattern, generally of stripes of "hit-or-miss" colors, with red where the little black squares show here. [#32]

The log cabin pattern. Again the hit-or-miss faded colored stripes with red, black, blue and white in each small square. [#32a]

TWO NOVA SCOTIAN RUGS

[35]

striking in general arrangement and type. Another *Scandinavian* fashion of floor covering persists hereabouts in the annual festivals of " Rush
bearing " in many Westmorland villages. This is usually in July when
the wild rushes are at their best and the children carry them in sheaves,
garlanded with flowers in a joyful procession.

' The old fashion was to lay rushes on the floor of the church to
keep the cold of the stone from dulling the feet of the faithful. One
old man near here remembers having to plait the rushes into mats as a
child. We do not grow the large " Juncus " rush in the North Country
meres, as in the fens and the Thames, where they used to make magnificent rush plaited mats, our rush is very small.

' I will make more definite enquiries as to history but I warn you
that any definite details are highly improbable. This has always been
a non-literate part of the world. It may be better in Scotland, here I
can get no local history beyond scrappy Parish registers and these do
not touch domestic arts. I will enquire of other people around Castle
Douglas.

' *Personally I hold to the conclusion that it is a very old affair —
quite 400 years old and probably older.'*

Miss Macbeth thus substantiates to a degree the report which I had
received from a friend that hooked rugs are found in *Scandinavia.* She
continues thus:

' I do not believe in copying old examples, one is always influenced
by them to some extent but as soon as the individual stops inventing and
relies on manufacturers' patterns the craft dies, all that is best in it, at
least, and my whole working aim is to stir up inventiveness, it matters
not in what material or craft, for I feel we have lost touch with the
holy spirit, because we have left too much to the machines. I am quite
sure your (i.e. American) hooked rugs hail from this part. I have
judged so many shows of Rural Industries up and down the country

Courtesy Messrs. Lord & Taylor, New York City, Bureau of Fashion and Decoration.

Of sheared wool, an excellent hooking, showing interesting abstract ornament, the semi-circles probably drawn on the basic fabric with a dinner plate. [#33]

[37]

and undoubtedly this is their home. You never see them in the South nor further north than I have told you.

' I will write the curator of the Bowes Museum at Bannard Castle and see if he knows anything about them.

Yours faithfully,
Anne Macbeth '

And later she writes,

' I have sent out the fiery cross! [1] and put letters *re* your quest into various local papers both here and north of the border, so I may be deluged with information of no great importance.

' Now as to your photographs (of rugs made in America which I sent to her) — " Most of ours are not so floral, but they vary extraordinarily, this is due largely to the fact that *most* of them are made of *old* materials and choice of colors has therefore been limited.

' The border of one of yours which I have marked " X " in the margin is a *very* common type here [2] but one fears to make statements as regards design because recently so many designs have been supplied by the trade.

' I have asked in my letters for photographs of any examples of over 150 years old. This may help us — but here, where all things seem old, age is not held in reverence as in your country and 150 years is really very new, still, I don't think people will have kept things like rugs for a very long time. The dales folk are fond of clean things and rugs are difficult to keep so pearly as they approve. I have more hopes of good examples from the *Scottish* districts.

Yours faithfully,
A. Macbeth '

[1] (The ancient signal of the Scots, to rouse the clans to war.)
[2] This was a rug of Mr. Oliver Williams' collection in Rockport, Mass., and had a border of scrolls like some of the old carvings referred to. See #4 and #5. It may have come from England originally.

[#34]

NOVA SCOTIAN DESIGNS [#35]

[39]

Thus one sees that besides giving us the very probable source of English hooked rug making, Miss Macbeth has opened a most interesting vein of thought as to the prevalence of scroll borders on eastern New England and Canadian rugs, for it seems almost certain that the myriad designs of scroll borders which have such a family likeness to each other, came from the carvings of early English or Tudor furniture abroad to which they even now, after decades and decades of change, bear a very close resemblance and these carvings find their prototypes in Scandinavian ornament. See for instance ' Small's Scottish Woodwork,' and in particular Plate 44 therein, where on the ears of the top rail of a chair back in Holyrood Palace is a scroll much like that on many of our Canadian-American hooked rugs. These scrolls are common on many pieces of English and Scottish furniture. This source for rug design is a logical one and would surely account for the constant repetition of scroll-bordered hooked rugs. The manufacturers of yarn finally seized on these scrolled rug patterns as salable and stamped thousands of them ready for the rug worker — who often bought yarn for rug making. Still further Miss Macbeth adds in a letter of February 2, 1928:

' All good housewives destroyed old rugs when they got grimy and no one seems to have any really old ones of any artistic value — none, that is to say, more than 150 years old — which does not count as very old here. For all that, I have pushed my enquiries further afield and find that my supposition as to a Norse origin seems to be substantiated, which is interesting —

' I have a long letter — not all relevant — from my Norse friend Benedicta Haslund, of Oslo. She has found that " loops have been made in olden days on ' Flensvaevnad ' i.e. double weaving, to make the rugs warm enough to use in place of skin rugs. These were used on the beds and were made on a woollen backing with woollen loops.

Fish scale motive, Eastern
Maine, now at Kentucket.
[#36]

Black and white harlequin
diamonds. [#37]

Collection of Miss Charlotte A. Kent

Part of early hooked carpet, Eastern Maine.
[#38]

Collection of Mr. and Mrs. Winthrop Kent, Buffalo, N. Y.

Very finely hooked. Pale yellow and violet tones.
It is like a tough piece of old tapestry. Nova
Scotia. [#39]

[41]

Close hooking and cropped, surface like Aubusson rug. Pattern more interesting than the Spanish and Italian motive from which it may have come. [#40]

Canadian maple leaf on black field of medallions stepped in parti-colored striped lines. A fine long runner. [#41]

[#42]

Collection of Mr. and Mrs. W. W. Kent

THREE NOVA SCOTIAN RUNNERS

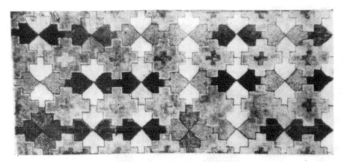

These two rugs illustrate well two of the good Canadian patterns, which were easily designed and worked, each unit could be filled with different remnants of colored cloth when not much of one kind was on hand. [#43]

Collection of A. Rubin, Esq., Boston, Mass.

This design was easily drawn by pushing a square card down in
equal distances to form the stepped medallions. [#44]

NOVA SCOTIAN RUGS

' " This weaving is called ' Rye weaving ' pronounced with the ' y ' like the German ' u ' and the ' e ' like our a, Rooa, but the ' oo ' or ' u ' very much modified. The word is believed to have come from the Anglo-Saxon Rŷhe — torn cloth. The first mention of ' Ryer ' in Norway and Sweden is about 1700 — as being part of the bed furnishings [3] and they are often mentioned as legacies in wills. But in Danish graves of the Bronze Age small pieces of woollen clothing, capes and cloaks and caps have been found with loops *hooked in* after the weaving was done."

' So far Miss Benedicta Haslund. But to my second confirmation. This from Miss Stout, inspectress of Rural Federations reporting on *Shetland* classes in hooked and looped rugs — She writes " For hundreds of years these rugs were made, each bride being required by tradition to have one or more as part of her dowry. They were used on the beds — not on the floor (as Miss Haslund says also) and were made in two halves and sewn together.

' " There were ' rug women ' who travelled about making rugs, receiving hospitality and meals in return for their work. The practice of making the rugs seems to have almost died out during the last generation. The ground was hand woven on Norwegian looms and though twenty years ago there were several weavers, to-day there is not one — the last weaver died six years ago. So it was impossible any longer to have hand woven grounds and the wool was sent to Brora to be woven there and except for being more regular than the hand-loom woven ground it is practically the same thing.

' " In olden times natural browns and home dyed wool only was used and in our present classes we are trying to do the same."

' Now Orkney and Shetland were entirely Norse islands, in fact Scotland only got them as part of the dowry of the Maid of Norway,

[3] They were so used in America (See #93 and #94).

Geometrical rug with a plain wall and formal American colonial furniture. [#45]

who was wrecked and the ship lost on her way to Scotland to be married to the king's son — see " Ballad of Sir Patrick Spens " — and the islands should rightly have been given back to Norway. But Miss Stout's information bears out Miss Haslund's and I feel justified in my own suspicion that Norse people introduced them (i.e. hooked rugs).

' I think you can safely say Norway was the place they hailed from and that argues an introduction to this part of the world — well — any time between the end of Roman occupation and 1066. You see this part of the world (Cumberland, Westmorland, etc.) was Scottish till Malcolm Can More defeated my notorious ancestor (Macbeth), when for some reason it was ceded to England probably because he (Malcolm) had to fight with a borrowed (English) army.

' Now I hope I have helped you to get a stage or two backward in the ancestry of hooked rugs.

' I learn that hundreds of the good wives of New England and eastern Canada are manufacturing " antique hooked rugs " hectically to supply the demand of collectors, so I fear many ardent collectors are being imposed on — or, rather, probably are getting sounder rugs than they realize. No matter, so long as the pattern is pleasing, for to my mind the idea in the design is the main thing.

I am yours faithfully,

Ann Macbeth '

Although from all this from Miss Macbeth it is certainly true that the origin was European, yet it is a fact that the art was taken up more widely and developed more artistically in America than elsewhere, so that to this continent and the islands belongs much credit for its advancement. This was undoubtedly due to the fact that the stock of the early settlers in America was of different nationalities and included both Latins and Irish, instinctively and generally art-loving.

Geometrical rugs in harmony with wall decoration. [#46]

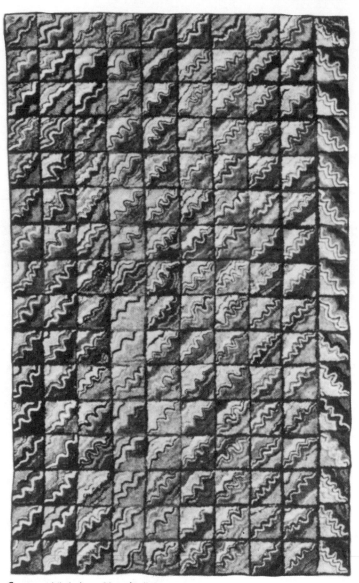

EARLY AMERICAN HOOKED CARPET

Composed of square tan and brown tiles; interestingly waved with
stripes of crimson, blue and ivory. 8′ 10″ x 5′ 4″ [#47]

CHAPTER III

The Simplicity of the Process

THE ENTIRE process of making a hooked rug is as follows; First, buy or make a hook. This may be made by filing down to a point a heavy wire nail of about ¼″ diameter, and either shaping it to a suddenly bent curve of about sixty degrees or so, as some pictures show it, or leaving the nail straight. On the point, fashion a hook like a crochet hook but with shank *hollowed out properly back of the catch above the point;* make a fine hook for a finely woven, and larger for a coarsely woven rug. It is best however for a beginner to make it of a medium size to catch strips of woolen or cotton cloth about one quarter of an inch wide, or more, according to the thickness of the cloth. Set this iron part in a handle so that the entire implement will not be over five inches long.

Never sew the cloth strips end to end as they will catch in pulling through the burlap or basic material. Then make a frame similar to an embroidery frame, but of two pieces (A & B) called spreaders, of maple or white wood, at least 1½″ thick by 2″ wide by 52″ long, with or without a ¼″ x 2″ groove made in each end to resist strain. Then make end pieces C & D ⅞″ x 2″ x 20″ to slide along on A & B or in the grooves made near the ends thereof. If the rug is to be large, make bars accordingly long, but small rugs are best for beginners. Mr. R. W. Burnham's practical frame is excellent as sold in Ipswich, Mass. He pushes the side pieces C & D through slots in the end pieces. Certain

Photo. by Richard Averill Smith

THE PASSAGE ROOM AT MILL FARM

Home of Mr. and Mrs. Edward C. Gude, Harrison, N. Y.   Woodland, Hutchinson river, and pond are visible from the

Courtesy of Messrs. Clifford & Lawton, N. Y.

In a room of this size a number of both floral and geometrical hooked rugs are admissible, but a braided rug seems always out of place near them. [#49].

workers advise fastening the corners of four plain pieces, without grooves, together with wooden or iron pins driven through holes to hold the frame rigid when the burlap is stretched, but it is difficult to stretch the burlap tightly and yet slip the pins of the shorter pieces into their corresponding holes in the ends of the two longer pieces. Clamps at the corners are easily moved for restretching from time to time.

The easiest and quickest way for those who can afford the small outlay is to buy a good frame and follow the directions. Then cut up a new potato or feed sack of burlap, or better, buy a piece of strong new burlap. A new coffee sack is a good basis for a strong, coarsely hooked rug. Next obtain the design of the rug in color on a small scale, and decide how large the full-size finished rug will be and stencil or draw it on the burlap in black or any good color. By tacking down the burlap after dampening it can be stretched smooth. After this, not before, hem the burlap all around, by turning under two and a half inches of it even with the outer edge or border of the design, with strong carpet thread or cotton twine, cutting out and sewing the turned-over part at corners to retain there only two thicknesses of burlap. Put frame together, pieces being called A-B-C-D. Attach the burlap to bar A by loops of strong twine set 2″ apart or, as by the Burnham method, to strong webbing tacked to A, and similarly fasten the other side to bar B and stretch it tightly from A to B, placing C and D in the grooves or slots of end pieces A and B. Then secure the corners of A, B, C and D with clamps at each corner of frame or, on the Burnham frame, with the pegs in holes as directed. If clamps are used they may be bought at any hardware or notion store for five or ten cents. Next, if very tight stretching is desired (in a homemade frame) secure the sides of the burlap by pieces of strong twine cut in separate loops and passed through the hem 1½″ or 2″ apart, each tied with a tight bowknot to bars C and D at each side of the frame. The frame may be made or

Photo. by J. W. Gillies, Inc., N. Y.

INTERIOR OF DINING ROOM. HOUSE OF THEODORE BODENWEIN, ESQ., NEW LONDON, CONN.

Showing effective use of geometrical hooked rugs with a trestle table, Lancashire chairs and wall boarding of a traditional early English character, so often used in early American colonial houses. (Courtesy of Frank J. Forster, Arch't N. Y., and of "House Beautiful.") [#50]

It would be hard to select a more appropriate geometrical hooked rug for this table and this room.

[#51]

bought large enough to hold the full size of burlap when stretched, and if so, do not roll it on the bar. In the smaller rugs this is preferable, but large rugs must be rolled, on one bar partly and then on to the opposite bar, as fast as done.

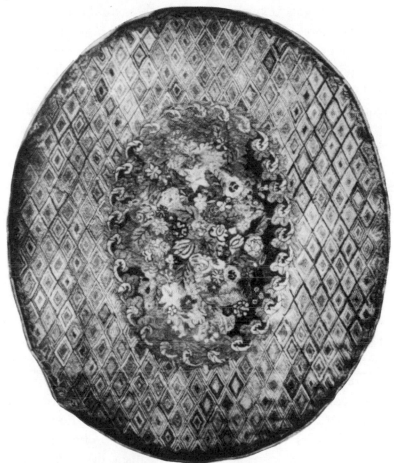

Courtesy of R. W. Burnham, Esq.

Good contrast of floral with geometrical designs. Probably of New Hampshire origin. A piece of great beauty. [#52]

[55]

Now take the hook in the right hand and a ¼" wide strip of woolen cloth of any moderate length in the left, which hold below the frame; thrust the hook down through the burlap, catching it on the cloth strip and drawing this up through the burlap. Leave the end of the strip standing above burlap. Push hook again down through the second mesh beyond and draw up a loop about ¼" high to wedge the first end from pulling out. Count two, or three, mesh openings away from second hole, according to the thickness of the cloth strip, then put the hook down through and pull carefully a loop of the strip up, and let it also stand ¼" or more above the burlap surface. Pull loops firmly and tightly over the hook each time before removing hook from loop. Repeat this process in every second or third mesh opening as you prefer, in the direction desired. The third opening is far easier and gives good results especially for a beginner. The second mesh opening makes a finer, closer woven rug but takes longer. Work now in general from the edge inward toward the rug center and *work the outline of the patterns first,* filling in the solid color effects when all the outlines are done; this prevents puckering. In making a woolen *clipped* rug, as some prefer, it is well to pull the loop a little higher every three inches or so of the line as worked and cut it off to height of lower loops already cut to help the final matting of the wool or felt. When a loose end is left standing, always begin work with the new strip by pulling it through the same hole to wedge in the loose end and clip off both later, even in a rug not otherwise clipped.

Cotton and woolen rugs are often clipped over the entire surface, but the former are thus apt to ravel. By some Prince Edward Island workers and others, the surface of a woolen rug is often modeled, or made high and low in relief to obtain realistic or modeled flower, foliage and border effects. These are not always objectionable when the rug is used for the hearth, but few are as beautiful as the tightly

From the Ives Collection, Danbury, Conn.

Small, but excellent detail. [#53]

Courtesy of Jas. M. Shoemaker Co., N. Y.

Good work in spite of pussy's (or Tom's)
coarse whiskers. [#53a]

THRESHOLD RUGS

[57]

drawn, unclipped level surface rugs, and their general use as rugs soon proves the idea of a raised or modeled surface illogical, unless made as curiosities. As rugs, they have not as good an excuse for being, as had Pinturriccio's modeled frescoes in Siena and Rome.

If making a long or wide rug, not stretched its full size at first but rolled up on one bar ready for working, when the rug is finished in one part across its full width, roll it up on A and stretch it taut again and proceed as before. When the rug is done, examine the front and back, clip any roughness off and secure the loose ends on both sides by sewing or wedging in more cloth strip with the hook.

Portable knockdown stand to support working frame. [#53b]

All this process is very simple, and has been done practically thus for a long time, but it requires attention and patience until proficiency is learned and then the work goes quite rapidly. Then also exact counting of holes is discarded, especially when filling in a pattern outline, and the eye and hand quickly select the proper thrusting places for the hook.

The frame may be easily supported on the backs of two chairs or on a chair and a window sill, but a stand to hold the frame makes the work a little easier and can be made, as has been devised by the writer, from $7/8''$ maple or cherry, birch, walnut, pine or white wood and the pieces framed into each other. It can be quickly taken apart for packing or transportation. This would appear when set up about as shown in plate here (#53b). By making various square holes and using four pins,

From the Ives Collection, Danbury, Conn.

[#54]

Courtesy of Mrs. E. O. Schernikow, N. Y.

Brought $475 at Am. Art Asso., N. Y., Feb. 6, 1930. A cluster of roses, lilies, and other flowers at the center, surrounded by a wreath of the same flowers on a brownish black field. Sheared. 6′ 3″. [#55]

two at each end of the cross of tie-bar X, inside and outside, the stand can be held rigid when the side pieces C and D of the frame are shifted in or outwards for small rugs as shown, or larger ones, according to whichever holes the pins are driven into. In case very large rugs are attempted (not desirable for beginners) larger frames and longer crossbars on frame are necessary, but narrow pieces of rug made on small frames were often in the old days sewed together to form a large rug.

The frame A, B, C and D is held up, on the stand, either at a height to work standing, which is restful, or at a sitting height, by movable hardwood pins about 1″ long. These pass into the sides of frame at E, F, and G, H either through holes bored at the top of the upright side pieces of stand, or through the ones lower down, for either standing or chair-height working. The pieces of the stand are made framed or jointed, either to glue together, or to leave as a portable ' knockdown ' stand.

In case a stain is desired to subdue the rawness of the wood, a little permanganate of potash in warm water may be applied, or raw or burnt umber and linseed oil, Indian red and a little black powder pigment mixed together in linseed oil will also give an excellent dull oid Colonial red which may be further improved by rubbing down in boiled linseed oil, or a simple finish in floor wax.

From Ives Collection, Danbury, Conn.
[#56]

Courtesy of Messrs. Flint & Kent, Buffalo, N. Y.
Fine Canadian design with modeled work in center. Probably
Canadian or Eastern Maine. [#57]

HOOKED RUG OF SHEARED WOOL

Valued at $15,000. A historic piece. Deep toned field, bluish and brownish black, flowers and leaves in natural colors. *Sizes: 14 feet x 14 feet 3 inches.* [#58]

CHAPTER IV

Suitable Materials and Dyeing

G OOD commercial burlap costs so little and is so strong and well woven that it is better to use it rather than old burlap after the first rug has been made. Early rugs were done on homemade linen, sugar, coffee and feed bags, cotton cloth, canvas, etc. As to cloth for hooking, yarn or smooth woolens are best for the beginner, the latter evenly cut into ¼″ wide strips by rolling and slicing with a very sharp knife or better still an old razor. Heavy strands of twisted woolen yarn are excellent, but even thick cotton or jute twine and candle wicking can be used. Rough cloth strips often bring good effects when parti-colored in stripes or with dots. This is advised for certain mosaic and wavy variegated backgrounds, queer flowers, etc. Old washed rags or newly dyed cloth, bought for the purpose and dyed at home, or red and blue flannels, old or artificially faded to secure antique tones are excellent. Waste green felting may be bought in strips and squares at the billiard table makers' at about one dollar a pound. At the city rag stores mixed cottons, remnants and scraps cost about twenty-five cents a pound and upwards but should be boiled or cleansed. Some stores now sell dyed cotton strips by the pound. Mrs. Albee at Pequaket, N. H., made her ' Abnakee ' rugs from unfinished twilled flannel, which she finally bought new in considerable quantities, as related in her interesting book. Old woolen and cotton or mill-rejected stockings are excellent in strips 1″ wide and there is nothing better when cut spirally round and round, and all cloth works better when cut evenly. Cotton cloth cut thus and not on the bias will make a beautiful unclipped rug, but wears flatter and dirtier than wool although often very beautiful in tone even when old, faded and worn.

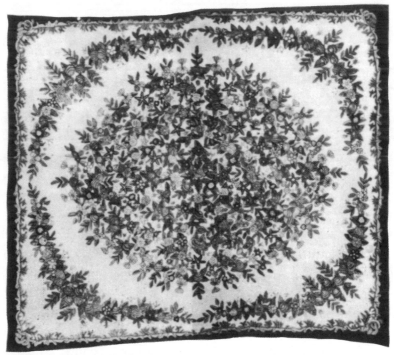

Courtesy of Mrs. E. O. Schernikow, N. Y.

Example of unusually minute floral pattern of recognizable flowers. [#59]

As to velvets and silks, they may be used for certain parts, but silk wears poorly and is not often found in good rugs, while velvet is somewhat expensive and hard to get in the form of rags. Jute and wool yarn are frequently used, especially in Canada and Scotland.

If one wishes to dye old or new materials, it is best to learn to make

MODELLED RUG, EARLY AMERICAN

Magnificent hooking on grayish tan base, borders of blue. Whole surface covered with gorgeous array of raised leaves of many lovely colors. Most important rug, at Glick sale, Feb. 6, 1924. *Size:* 4′ 4″ x 3′ 1″. [#60]

[65]

dyes and rely on Charles E. Pellew's book 'Dyes and Dyeing,' or Mrs. Helen R. Albee's 'Abnakee Rugs,' or Elizabeth Calvert Hall's 'Hand Woven Coverlets,' or Amy Mali Hick's 'The Art of Handmade Rugs.' Some of these books give scientifically tested recipes, others the method and recipes of those people who experimented with the grasses, leaves, roots, bark and nuts that the woods and fields afforded, as did the Indian, and later the women of Colonial days. To try the dyeing recipes is not advisable for beginners who can obtain cloth already dyed. There is a certain rather romantic interest, however, in reading of the primitive research and use of natural products, made and described by the unlettered but tireless and determined experimenters of early days in America. They give the directions in a few words of forceful, if primitive, English.

In the late Mrs. Elizabeth Lounsbery's article in *Harper's Bazar,* 'The Native American Rug,' she says:

'The principal home dyes of the period were derived from hemlock bark, yellow hickory, peach leaves, walnut or spruce bark. Golden-rod was also employed for making yellow, set with copperas; also onion skins, set with alum, and sumac for soft gray.'

Quoting Mr. Douglas Leechman in an excellent article in the March 1930 issue of *The American Home,* entitled 'The Magic Dyes of Olden Days' it may be further said that 'The following lists of plants which can be used direct, without any previous preparation or mordanting of the goods to be dyed, does not pretend to be complete, nor are the dyes of equal value. Experiments should always be made before risking any valuable cloth in little-known dye baths.

' *Red:* Alder, bedstraw, bloodroot, cedar, cranberry, dogwood, elm, grape, gromwell, hemlock, hooked-crowfoot, lamb's-quarters, maple, sorrel, spruce roots, sumac, tamarack.

' *Yellow:* Alder, barberry, beech, blue beech, crab apple, golden-

A delightful New England specimen of conventional floral design. [#61]

rod, goldenseal, goldthread, hickory, marsh marigold, oak, poplar, prickly ash, quercitron, sassafras, sumac, sunflower, touch-me-not, willow.

' *Black:* Alder, poison ivy, sumac, walnut.

' *Orange:* Alder, bittersweet, dodder, sassafras, touch-me-not, willow.

' *Green:* Ash, hound's-tongue, mint, smartweed, walnut (young), yellow adder's-tongue.

' *Purple:* Blueberry, elderberry, huckleberry.

' *Brown:* Alder, butternut, oak, walnut.

' *Blue:* Grape, larkspur, oak, spruce bark, sycamore, toadflax.

' It will be seen that some plants, such as alder, are listed as giving more than one color. In most cases this depends on the length of time that the goods are boiled in the dye or the strength of the decoction. In other cases the nature of the goods to be dyed will affect the color.

' Most of these dyes of olden days were prepared in very simple ways, generally by boiling the goods with parts of the dye-bearing plant.

' The butternut was prepared by boiling the inside bark and the nut rinds with the wool which was to be woven into homespun. Sometimes the brown was varied by adding walnut bark, with black as a result. This was one of the best known and most popular dyes and so many of the Confederate soldiers were dressed in homespun colored with butternut dye that the name " Butternuts " stuck to them for many years.'

Therefore, after some little proficiency has been reached in the technique of hooking, it will be found very interesting not only to try certain of the old dyeing recipes, but also to make experiments along the same lines with entirely different barks, roots, leaves and blossoms. But dyeing to be successful must be carefully done and the proportions

Made about seventy-five years ago at Peterborough, N. H.
Size: 6 feet 7 inches x *9 feet 10 inches.* [#62]

of ingredients as well as the incidents of the whole operation carefully and specifically noted, otherwise it may not be possible to secure the same result twice in succession.   One thing is certain, the beginner

Courtesy of Mr. and Mrs. E. C. Gude   *Photo. by Richard A. Smith, N. Y.*

ROOM AT MILL FARM, HARRISON, N. Y.

With two floral rugs of delicate tones and workmanship and a braided one.   [#63]

will get better results by using pale or faded colors throughout a rug rather than very brilliant new tones.

It is well to be sure of enough material for each intended color surface, before beginning a rug.   It is true that some excellent, indeed surpassingly fine rugs, have been made from small batches of cloth, one

Photo by Walter Westervelt

ACADIAN FRENCH, NOVA SCOTIA, OF GREAT BEAUTY

A wool yarn hooked rug, 2 feet 6 inches x 5 feet 3 inches, with soft tan field, on which appears a grapevine border in greens and tan, surrounding a broken wreath of old-time flowers of natural colors. [#64]

used when another color gave out, until a desirable oriental effect was secured, even if not known by this name to the maker, but, if this is to be done, a pattern of small details should be prepared, although on backgrounds or 'fields' many varying colors may be wisely used.

Try the strips before cutting many, to be sure that you have made them the proper width for easy working and for final effect on the finished rug surface. To calculate how much will be needed before beginning a rug estimate that one square foot of rug surface will use up a dozen or less times as many square feet of cloth, depending on the thickness of the cloth and width of strips. Carpet ravelings are also available and suitable if thickly twisted and some rugs are made entirely of this and of chenille, but the latter is usually sewed on, not hooked.

Many excellent heavy yarns for hooked rug making are now on the market at reasonable prices and as the dyes are good in tone and the colors are fast it is easier, far easier for the beginner at least, to use these than rags although what has been said above as to the charm of old and often faded household materials will be appreciated when the worker tries to secure the finer shades and blendings so often seen in old rugs. To be sure, it is time, sun and wear that give to them their chief color value, but by study, even by making drawings in crayon and pastel, or in actual rug making, excellent harmonies can be obtained.

It is interesting and well to remember that old household cloth remnants added to hand-woven pieces old or new, hooked on hand-woven fabrics as a foundation, often by their very limitations, or originality in color, gave to the older rugs an almost uncopyable charm. This is because, as said, a small supply of different kinds of cloth led to necessary sudden changes in color or in tone, the homespun or home-dyed colors being also charming in themselves. This subject, however, leads naturally to the design itself as treated in the next chapter.

CHAPTER V

Source, Suggestion and Decadence of Designs
Certain Late Utensils

EVERY earnest collector knows that the hooked or ' drawn-in ' or
' pulled-in ' rugs, as they are called in different parts of New England and Canada, vary greatly in design. In early days many of the
patterns were suggested to isolated rug makers, by natural forms;
leaves, ferns, grasses, garlands, flowers, fruit, birds, beasts, fish, etc.
Even the effects of sky and sea, field and mountain scenery were attempted in crude form, often with fair results. Seafaring folk or those
dwelling near the sea, often represented the compass, capstan, anchor
and even boats and ships, shell and fish forms. Houses, especially
farmhouses and homesteads, huts, camps and settlements, views of
towns, are sometimes pictured, often indescribably bad in color and
drawing, sometimes well done and of interest. Mr. Burnham who
has probably seen more hooked rugs in thirty-five years than any one
man, gives a list of designs which he has found. This includes geometrical, floral, animal, landscape motives and combinations of these,
and it refers to the dog, horse and cat as the most common animal
forms, also noting ducks, geese, cows, bulls, swans and cygnets, deer,
poultry, sheep, foxes, lions and leopards, flowerpots, baskets and vases
of flowers as quite common. Sometimes one finds rugs showing people,
interiors, fireplaces, clocks, etc. In fact the range of design seems in-
finite, and yet in abstract geometrical patterns we can trace varying
repetition.

[73]

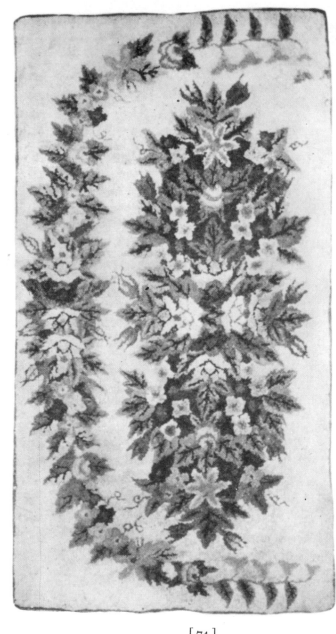

Courtesy of "Harper's Bazar" and Miss Elizabeth H. Rowe, Inc., N. Y.   Photo. by Walter Westervelt

Hearth hooked rugs are distinguishable by their three-sided design, as is shown in this example.   *3 feet x 5 feet 7 inches.* Purple, tan, green, red and gray prevailed, with dark green veining in the foliage, as the colorings against a natural wool ground. [#65]

Courtesy of American Carpet and Upholstery Journal

ACADIAN RAISED FLOWER HOOKED RUG

A marvelous example of old hooking entirely executed in home-spun worsted. *Size: 5 feet x 2 feet 10 inches.*

[#66]

As to other patterns from suggestion, wall papers, textiles, oriental rugs, oil cloths, early bed coverlets on which hooking was in early use, and even other rugs of Spain and oriental countries and European china, Chinese boxes and tea chests, often furnished inspiring help by their decorations. One of the most remarkable small rugs in a private collection came from Westchester County, N. Y., and is so like a pure Persian design in scheme and color as to force the belief that the maker not only knew but deeply appreciated oriental rug design if not Persian art itself, yet the rug possibly was made on a farm in New York State and differs from any I have seen. The suggestion which it gives, of the possible variations on this crude theme, is very valuable.

Often the designs are hideous beyond belief and of these it is usually hard to trace the origin. Often too they are of rare beauty, made evidently by people who not only knew flower forms and used color combinations with great skill and refinement, but also must have possessed much of the patience of the oriental. Some of these makers' names are known and they were chiefly New Englanders and Canadians. One rug shown to me by Miss Elizabeth Rowe of New York was made by a lady she knew. The hook for this was of a flat piece of ivory only two inches long (#1) and the hooked point very small to suit the very delicate quality of the rug, which was of wool, excellent in design and execution and of great artistic and intrinsic value. The maker was evidently inspired by a love of flowers and a knowledge of French design.

In fact so wide is the range of possible design in hooked rugs and so surpassingly effective are the results that it is not hard to account for the fascination the art has exercised not only on the housewife of the lonely farmhouse, but on artists, hard-headed business men, bankers, sea captains and men and women of other professions and walks in life, who each sought inspiration as temperament suggested.

Collection of Elizabeth H. Rowe, Inc., N. Y.

Early New England, Maine or New Hampshire, wool, unsheared, roses of delicate hues on an ivory field.

[#67]

Traditional patterns are many, symbolic patterns, as already stated are few, and religious and fraternity emblems rare, even in many large collections. In the first-mentioned class, the patterns which grew from the utilization of scraps of cloth are the most common and sometimes quite beautiful.

The basket-weave patterns are of various kinds, wherein strips of various colors seem to pass over and under alternate blocks of strips running in an opposite direction and the blocks are outlined often in black or brown. This motive is very ancient and dates of course from the discovery of weaving and basketry. The ' hit-or-miss,' kaleidoscopic arrangement of lines in quadrangular and block forms also shows considerable ingenuity and resource, but the finest and most valuable suggestion made by some of the early makers, is found in rugs where the background and pattern together, or separately in contrast, are done in delicate shadings of the same color, *the lines put in to follow around the various patterns,* just as map makers often emphasize the water lines around the coasts. Whether this came from a knowledge of mosaic patterns or the subconscious repetition of maps made in childhood, with their coast lines emphasized by parallel boundary lines, when the copyist went to the little red schoolhouse at the crossroads, or the process of rug making itself suggested the ease of bounding one line of the material by another to push the slack of the burlap evenly toward the center, whatever the cause, the final effect is often surprisingly good in softening the outlines of patterns, making also an interesting wavy background, and is logical and sometimes very beautiful.

Those who have studied ancient mosaics know how the old mosaic craftsmen, oriental, Roman, Early Christian and Italian, appreciated and used this same idea of following one line of background by another around the pattern. This grew possibly at first from the ease of the operation, which obviated too frequent mosaic cutting, but it led,

Embroidered Rug of late eighteenth or early nineteenth century.   Worked on a linen ground with fine wool yarn.

Size: 60 inches x 30 inches.   [#68]

in the hands of an artist, to great beauty of effect. It is to be seen in much of the ancient mosaic and is illustrated in a pattern (#78), from the Baptistry in Ravenna. This method is emphasized here by the writer because the best unclipped hooked rugs have the effect of good mosaic, in fact they are *mosaics in cloth,* and long ago certain hooked rugs were called 'mosaics' in England. Whether coarse or fine, and even when matted down by 'felting' or 'matting' as in the woolen rugs after constant use, they give not only the rich effect of a mosaic in pattern but an added variation of line and softness of gradation in color. This effect many marble mosaics do not give, but, as has been said, certain Byzantine and Early Christian ones do, and not only in the Baptistry and other notable buildings at Ravenna but elsewhere in Italy, North Africa and the Orient. The study of mosaics in general, especially the Byzantine patterns and colors, helps amazingly in hooked rug making and is advisable.

These suggestions of the possibilities which lie in treating the design of a rug as a mosaic, and in reviving the Persian idea of small bits of color, used in both abstract and conventionalized floral design, are, whatever the origin, two of the most valuable hints which early hooked rug makers have given us, and cannot be too carefully noted. In the interest of modern rug designers, it is well to repeat that the path which these two suggestions indicate is the one which will lead to great beauty and it is to be hoped they may be in time exploited by Americans. It is because the hooked rug has never been developed to the limit along these lines that this is said with emphasis. *Realistic* forms of flower and landscape, etc., have indeed been so developed and the results, as in other arts, are usually not of the greatest value, although outlining with double, triple and more lines as above described does help to destroy the irritating smugness of realistic foliage and flowers, and secures a certain value of conventional quality.

Courtesy of " Antiques Magazine "   FREE FLORAL DESIGN, NEW ENGLAND.   [#69]

UNSHEARED WOOL, NEW ENGLAND.   [#70]

ACADIAN MODELED OR RAISED PATTERN

Field unclipped, with clipped and raised flowers and scrolls. All of woollen yarn, except field of rags. Excellent technique.

[#71]

As to varieties of texture, which produce different effects according to their surfaces, the unclipped rug, wherein the loops are drawn tightly to a low and even height and so left, is in the opinion of many critics, the most beautiful and the most durable, as well as the most difficult to make. Clipping, in such rugs, is confined to the loose ends which occasionally occur in all hooked rugs. This method is, among old rugs, often found to have been done on a homemade, hand-woven basic fabric.

The deterioration in the design of the hooked rug came with the commercializing of the design itself by the stamping or stenciling of bad stock designs on burlap for the trade. These were not always bad, but often execrable. Had they been done by able designers or from study of good old rugs, the general level of rug design would have been raised, but as it is, they have, although producing more makers of rugs, often tended to lower in quality the general average of design.

It is very noticeable in collecting rugs that many designs, wholly or in part original with the farmer's wife or children, have an especial naïve, æsthetic character. As in foreign peasant art, some chance effect, or some sudden inspiration as the work progressed, has given a certain remarkable quality to the homemade design. For instance, the use of familiar patterns, such as hearts in so-called ' wedding ' or ' courtship ' rugs, triangles, stars, interlaces, and circles, or a background in wavy lines of different colors of nearly the same tone, or again the outlining of certain patterns and nonemphasis of others, the soft gradations of the same color in pattern or background, all these and some other touches were not easily suggestible in a rough stamped or stenciled design bought at the village store. For instance, certain rugs illustrated (#67, 69, 75, 77, 79, 81), could hardly have been produced by following a shop design.

Miss Alice Van Leer Carrick says in the catalog of the Wettleson

Made on coarse hand woven linen.   The old rose tints are beautiful.   [#72]

Sale, at the Anderson Galleries, New York, ' It is just this vivid personal quality I want to stress, for, in some way, it makes them akin to the direct craftsmanship of the furniture. That's why I hate what the old countrywomen hereabouts call "boughten patterns." These completely lack the naïve spontaneity which women, working by the fireside on snowbound afternoons, or men in the long hours of winter evenings, were able to create upon their canvases, which were strips of stretched burlap, with colors of home-dyed pieces of cloth and skeins of yarn. They reflected the life around them: the cat sleeping on the hearth, their memories of gold and crimson autumn, the blues of the *faïence* upon the tall mantel.' Yes, many of them had or knew *faïence*.

Of the texture of various rugs, one can only learn the effect by study of examples, and this study is of great value to the rug maker, whether he can determine the respective methods or not.

In the older rug it is noticeable that certain patterns are found often repeated in certain localities. This is due undoubtedly to the fact that people met occasionally in ' bees ' to work together and so compared patterns and borrowed ideas. Thus raised or modeled rug surfaces are common in New Hampshire, Prince Edward Island and Nova Scotia; block and basket-weave patterns in New Brunswick, ' hit or miss ' line patterns, and certain geometrical and ' tile ' patterns in Nova Scotia, animals of a certain kind in known parts of Maine and Canada, and so on. Sad to say, however, the effect of the bad, shop design is seen almost everywhere, and expert rug makers to-day in many outlying communities would welcome and probably buy good designs or suggestions in form and color from people who could furnish them. This might be done even through good local shops, and to the best advantage thus. The vital need is that the design itself should be logically good and therefore not heedlessly or ignorantly designed by the origi-

Interesting because of the scalloped and wavy corners where sometimes bad scrolls lie in wait.   [#73]

nator, but it results best of all if the maker of rugs makes his own designs, or varies the patterns which he buys.

One may say that it is not always to be desired that modern designers should try to make naïve designs or to repeat the primitive quaintness of many of the simple farmhouse rugs. Some of the most interesting and valuable early hooked rugs show considerable knowledge and lack the primitiveness so often overprized. Indeed there are early hooked rugs which are made on much the same pattern lines as those of good oriental knotted rugs, and with the evident knowledge of building up tone effects by different shades of respective colors. Even the emphasis of small dots of brilliant color was understood and employed by early makers who either knew from observation or by instinct how to proceed. It would be excellent practice in making, to copy exactly, at least once, the best small antique hooked rug obtainable. ' Copiez, copiez, mais toujours copiez juste.'

Modern designers can safely work in any of the ways which will make beautiful rugs, irrespective of school or nationality, and without repeating early American quaint forms, colors and technique, can apply their own knowledge and talent to develop the possibilities of hooking in directions not yet exploited to the full, as suggested in knotted Chinese and Japanese examples. It is only fair to say that while many stamped or shop designs were bad, resulting in realistic effects, yet there were good ones sold, and poor ones were improved upon by gifted workers either in fine coloring or correction of ugly outlines, while age always toned down the obtrusiveness of both patterns and colors.

In 1891 a pattern book in color was issued by E. Ross and Co., Toledo, Ohio, for use with their ' Novelty Machine,' in outline something like a small mandolin and of two pieces of wood sliding by each other, something like the ' Burr ' implement. The cloth strip or yarn was fed to a needle and punched through the burlap. Mr. Caswell

In the rug, 2 *feet* 6 *inches* x 5 *feet*, shown above, the grapevine, a popular motif in hooked rug design, provides the green foliage colorings outlining the center flower panel, in the pattern, against a white background. [#74]

2 *feet* 6 *inches* x 5 *feet*, with design in relief. Varicolored flowers, with scrolls in tan on a cream. [#75]

TWO RUGS IN ACADIAN MANNER

Hooked in New Hampshire and hardly used since the early part of the nineteenth century. Flowers modeled in pronounced relief.

Barrie of Scarsdale, N. Y. owned a rug showing lions and palm trees which is one of the designs in the book. Horses, dogs, cats, sheep and deer were also depicted therein most primitively as to colors.

Later Mr. John E. Garrett of Burlington, Vt., published ' Rug or Mat Patterns ' of various sorts in which cats and kittens, dogs, doves, interlaces and flowers are shown and are much like the earlier pattern books in general character. These may still be selling. He also shows a larger and a smaller hook. Rugs from these designs are undoubtedly still extant. A certain firm, E. S. Frost and Company, also issued colored designs and the Jas. M. Shoemaker Co. Sale Catalog shows, in (#186) one from their book.

Ross's ' Novelty Machine ' certainly made excellent rugs, technically speaking, and is still in use. I believe that it, or a similar one, the ' Susan Burr hook,' is sold now. In some of these pattern books certain designs, alike in general idea, seem to have been handed on as favorites from one issue to another but the Ross book is the best of the nineteenth century books that I have yet seen.

Surely however much we criticize all these pattern books on account of certain badly designed and carelessly printed suggestions, we must allow that they did encourage the art and were often improved upon by rug makers. The firms that published them deserve credit for having often assisted isolated workers who had little knowledge of design, but great desire to work and even at times remarkable inspiration. It is safe to say that a few of the best hooked rugs of New England are very like some of the American book patterns in general arrangement. Whether the book patterns followed these rugs or the rugs these patterns we shall never know, but my own belief inclines to the first supposition, because the pattern and colors both indicate French art and possibly Acadian French rugs from Nova Scotia as the source of inspiration.

IN ACADIAN STYLE

Black bordered hooked rug, 2 *feet* 4 *inches* x 4 *feet* 10 *inches* with design modeled in high relief, and executed in brilliant colors, against an ivory field. [#76]

Courtesy of Caswell Barrie, Esq., N. Y., Nov. 15, 1923

LARGE ANTIQUE HOOKED RUG

Very interesting old piece with all-over design of white medallions each with an apricot-colored flower and four gray leaves. Black and gray mottled ground. [#77]

Size: 7 feet 9 inches x 5 feet 8 inches.

Whether the use of any form of machine needle for hooking rug patterns always results in too great uniformity I cannot say. There are unclipped antique hooked rugs of great beauty which were evidently made by a more exact method than by the simple crochet form of hand hook and the designs seemed original with the worker. I have also seen execrable rugs evidently made by the latter process so that one comes to believe that personality and skill play the most important part in hooking, whether by hook or a fed-punching or hooking needle of any kind.

Lately there has come to the writer's notice the Bluenose Rug Hooker, that is possibly a comparatively modern invention. The claim made for this is that it is a rapid working needle or implement that insures a firm, even nap for a yarn rug by making all loops uniform. This is called by the maker a hooker, but, I would say, is of the 'brodding' type of implement, descended from the old 'brod' (brad) or 'prod' made of wood, bone or metal and used in England, Scotland and elsewhere many years ago.

The 'Bucilla' rug is well made by a patent form of hooker which may be obtained as well as the rugs at several large department stores.

Mosaic in Baptistry, Ravenna, Italy. Showing mosaic lines of one color following around another color. [#78]

Collection of Caswell Barrie, Esq., N. Y.

ANTIQUE HOOKED RUG

A fine old piece of unusual type, with floral design in beautiful tones of blue and yellowish tan. The entire center field filled with a large cluster of roses and buds with large blue leaves. Black border. *Size: 5 feet 3 inches x 2 feet 5 inches.*

[#79]

CHAPTER VI

*Classification of Designs and Rugs Contemporary with
Hooking in America*

WHILE it is manifestly impossible to date and classify exactly the overwhelming varieties of design in American hooked rugs which gradually come to a collector's notice, it is in a measure practicable to group them under various heads, separating somewhat the old from the new, the Victorian possibly from other kinds, and so note the characteristics of many and the tendency of others. They may be divided in America into four kinds as respects age or date of making, and in general it is a good plan to classify them as follows in periods, i.e. *Antique* 1775–1825; *Early* 1825–1875; *Late* 1875–1900; *Modern* 1900–1923, etc. I have only seen a few rugs which I could class as made about 1780–90 and one is (#128). Here the peculiar form of the eagle copied from our early coins and the discs taken from early Dutch paintings on Pennsylvania barns may well bring it within that period. The *process* is the same however and the basic material the same (cotton or linen), as in (#12) herein illustrated and as in (#4) and others.

One can, as shown farther on, make some prophecy as to what the handicraft will produce and what its artistic and even commercial future will be. For although the art primarily flourished in spite of any considerable help from the commercial side, other than the inconsiderable price which the rugs, when new, brought in passing from maker

[95]

ANTIQUE HOOKED RUG WITH RELIEF WORK

Pale gray, lavender, moss-green, and fawn. Border of elaborately scrolled leaves in raised and moulded work. Center with well-designed flower basket with flower-spray on each side. [#80]   *Size: 4 feet 5 inches x 2 feet 4 inches.*

Collection of Caswell Barrie, Esq., N.Y.

ACADIAN TYPE ANTIQUE WOOLEN HOOKED RUG IN RELIEF DESIGN

Elaborate and finely worked piece with raised and moulded flower designs in pastel colors on the white center. Border of tan acanthus scrolls. Outer border in black [#81]

Size: 5 feet 2 inches x 2 feet 6 inches.

to neighbor or friend, yet to-day the commercial value is considerable and steadily increases, not only in the case of old rugs but actually of rugs now produced. As an instance of this latter fact, the owner of a New Jersey tea house designed and made his first hooked rug not many years ago. It was like nothing that he had ever done before either in technique or design, in fact, he let himself go, so to speak. A wealthy customer asked the price and the owner sold it for $300.00. As to the very finest old rugs, the auctions give the most reliable valuations obtainable, and these are sometimes equal to if not more remarkable than the value just mentioned above, and sometimes inexplicably low, though not often thus. A modern, fine, closely woven basket-pattern rug made by modern workers by the Hearthstone Studios, New York City and as beautiful and well made as any ancient rug, measuring about 9' x 14' brought four figures in New York, for a New England seashore house, I was told.

Beginning with simpler designs, the 'block' or 'basket-weave' (#32) already alluded to in Chapter IV, consisting of squares or features filled with stripes running at right angles to other stripes in adjacent squares or forms, is one of the most frequent geometrical and probably one of the oldest patterns in its many different phases. Next comes the 'wave' or zigzag like old Venetian glass and the 'inch square' design. All these were and are now made in New England and Canada, but are commoner in New Brunswick perhaps than elsewhere. More complicated and varied, though also early, is the so-called 'log-cabin' pattern (#33) from its fancied resemblance to logs piled up in a cabin wall. This is also called the 'Lincoln log-cabin' in one form. There are many changes rung on this, some of the quadrangular spaces formed by it being filled with flowers realistic or conventional. Wherever hooked rugs have been made in America it seems that some form of this was known and the motive is susceptible of endless variations. Perhaps one great reason for the popularity of this, also of the ' box ' or ' basket-weave ' and of certain simpler designs, was that scraps of different cloth could so easily be used in them. The final effect thereby obtained even improved on what would have been

AMERICAN CIRCA 1800

Rare fluctuating finely hooked blush orange field occupied by a Willard mantel clock between two pots of flowers within a floral oval wreath. Executed in blues, rose-pinks, ivory, tawny-browns and grays. [#82]
Size: 4 feet 8 inches x 3 feet 3 inches.

the result had one color been used all through a certain repeated part of the design. Generally speaking all designs which consist of a repetition of a certain unit or motive are naturally the commonest and oldest, being easier patterns to hand from one worker to another and also easier to draw on the burlap, and to execute. The writer has a ' log-cabin ' rug in two pieces which covers seven by ten feet of a dining-room floor;

it consists of a motive which is made with small lengths of cloth and is never repeated in quite the same colors (#32a).

Returning to the 'wave' design which is of oriental origin, it is remarkable how effective this simple pattern becomes in its varied forms. Sometimes it is made in a plain zigzag repeated in varying colors, sometimes each row of bends, or V's, is separated from the next row by dark lines of brown or black running the full length of the rug. Then again the V is varied by change from an acute to a flatter V or wedge shape as it passes from one part to another.

The 'shell' or imbricated pattern (#36) was almost as popular as the 'log-cabin' and is often found both as a pattern and as a background on old rugs in Eastern Maine and New Brunswick as well as in Nova Scotia and Prince Edward Island. It was told me by a rug maker of that island that an English clergyman brought the 'shell' pattern there with him from the old country, but of course the motive is a very old one in the history of design. One of its variations is used as a border like the old hoop or arch forms of the twig-made fences for garden beds. The round or top of the hoop points into the middle of the rug as a rule. A slight variation of the shell is known as 'lamb's tongue.'

The lattice or trellis seems never to have been as popular as the other simple forms already mentioned, but is often seen in stamped 'store designs' consisting of one or two crossed sticks or branches on which realistic flowers are twining. The effect is always bad when it is so used, but an all-over trellis or lattice design is often excellent, when flowers and colors are good.

The interlace of various forms is often found, sometimes used as a border and sometimes as a pattern running throughout the rug. In simple form it frequently makes oriental shaped spaces alternately of

BARK MERMAID HOMEWARD BOUND

Evidently a sailor's work on ship or shore. [#83]

This repetition of the same ship would hardly have been done by a sailor, but perhaps by his wife or sweetheart. [#84]

solid quiet color and flower filled, or with a spray of flowers on repeated backgrounds of white or color.

Geometrical forms such as stars, circles (#18), squares (#47),
diamonds (#52), queer medallions (#77, 107) and innumerable
forms are not uncommon and when executed with varied backgrounds
of low tones are very beautiful.

Collection of Mrs. E. O. Schernikow

THE BRIG AUTUMN

White against a blue and mauve background.
Size: 3 feet 9 inches x 2 feet 5 inches. [#85]

One of the finest rugs in the collection of the writer has in pattern
delicate black stems carrying pale pink roses on a field of intricately
worked light tones. The entire effect is purely Persian in character.
The same maker, a New Brunswick woman, had made many rugs of
this general and decidedly original excellence but varying in character,
indeed her work was of the most interesting sort as to design, although

in technique surpassed by less original designers. Two of her designs are shown in illustrations (#16, 17).

Courtesy of Jas. M. Shoemaker Co.

EARLY AMERICAN

Oblong blue field, curiously banded in tans at lower portion and occupied by an ivory and yellow goblet of red-crimson flowers. Borders chevroned in blues, ivories, tans and crimson, interrupted with cartouche corners. Black guards. [#86]   *Size: 3 feet 9 inches x 3 feet.*

When we reach floral design in the classification of American hooked rugs we are impressed with the fact that an exact knowledge of flower, leaf, bud, and branch did not always produce the most interesting floral design. Very often the crudity and simple treatment of a flower composition is part of its charm, provided that a good color arrangement is not lacking. Some of the strangest flowers grow on hooked rugs, probably merely the half-remembered effect of grouping and color once seen by an untrained eye, which nevertheless enjoyed form and color.

Mrs. Carrick says, ' Nowhere else, except in the pages of the medieval miniaturists who worked with precisely the same feeling, do flowers bloom in the same profusion of unpremediated art. I have just been examining an illustration of " Le Roman de la Rose," and, if I showed it to you, covering the figures with my hand, and you saw just the blossoms, you'd swear that you were looking at a North-Country hooked-rug. I fancy they must have some quality of eternal-ness.'

Take for instance illustration (#3) of a rug from Eastern Maine showing red roses, pink buds, green and brown leaves in a brown receptacle, on a white field with a ' hit-or-miss ' border of yellows, reds, blacks, blues, etc. Its very childlike drawing and coloring are delightful. Its directness appeals at once. Moreover its arrangement fills the panel beautifully and the colors to-day are almost as fresh as when hooked in by the then young French girl who made it fifty or more years ago. The same general criticism is true of (#20).

One of the most interesting small rugs known to me belongs to Mrs. Hayden Richardson and is at the Sign of the Motor Car at Dennis, Cape Cod, Massachusetts. It is so good that I venture to give here the colors with the design (#15). The vase is dark brown, the general field is ivory, vine stem dark green, darker leaves are dark and pale green, light fan-shaped leaves each side of vase are white with blue outline; the two flowers at center are orange colors in red outlines, the tulips green with red stripes, grapes are lavender, red and purple; of four flowers at right of tulips three are yellow and blue and lower one a

A mosaic, unsheared, shaded geometric example, possibly from Eastern Maine or New Brunswick. [#87]

red outline. All colors are softened by age and wear and the entire effect is of great beauty. This probably came from Maine or New Hampshire though found in Massachusetts. To reproduce it exactly would be impossible. It hangs on the wall where it well deserves to be.

Very original and handsome are some of the unclassifiable abstract designs such as hexagons, etc., with quadrants of circles in the corners in indescribable colors. Such a one is from Cape Cod. Also very strange is the one with nine white and red circular wheel patterns on a dull gray field, from Maine (#14). Also one with stepped octagons filled in with various colors (#32a).

Probably most of the scroll patterns which are frequently seen are in origin of very early Tudor date or earlier and many are from shop or stamped patterns. Some are interesting, some beautiful and many late ones are very bad. One, of red and yellow scrolls on a dark field is from its very roughness of drawing good. The scrolls are like sea horses and it is of Nova Scotia origin. The scroll pattern has evidently been a great favorite; probably, as stated before, it came from Scandinavian Scots carvings and was often combined with realistic flowers and with more conventional forms. Several are illustrated in (#12, 27, 57, 61, 72, 93).

Mr. E. C. Gude of Mill Farm, Mamaroneck, N. Y. in his very interesting collection has a wonderfully fine rug about 5′ x 7′ (#133). This is French in general character.

Of original abstract design including scrolls, rugs by two New Brunswick makers are most commendable. They are of colors high in key. The peacock and scrolls is not so rich, but fully as ambitious and very strange and interesting in spite of the queer form of the peacock, who sports pink legs. (#118).

One of the finest combinations in rug design of geometric, imbricated and conventional flower designs is in the circular rug owned by

EARLY AMERICAN RAISED FLORAL HOOKED RUG

Fine heavy hooking. Ivory field with very beautiful raised floral bouquet in crimsons, pink, blues, lavenders and greens. The field scrolled with crimson leaves. Black borders. [#88]

Size: 3 feet 11 inches x 2 feet 3 inches.

Horns of Plenty holding large flowers in crimson, rose, and ivory on a light brown field, with scalloped border in the same shades. Hooked on *homespun* canvas.

Size: 4 feet 9 inches x 2 feet 11 inches. [#89]

Mr. John C. Spring of Boston (#29). This is the work of a good designer, no tyro in knowledge of patterns. It is fine in composition, color arrangement and technique, briefly a remarkable production and one of the best of the known rugs of New England collections. I should say it came from Maine or New Hampshire. It lay, when photographed, on a flat granite bowlder which slightly distorts it from its perfectly circular form when flat.

Others combining conventional flowers are shown in (#19, 26, 28).

An oval centered rug with a flower border filling in the C. H. Allen Collection, is of great beauty in color and a splendid example of conventional treatment of flower forms.

Realistic flowers are attempted in numbers of the rugs of the Victorian period already referred to. Many made at that time are found in which color and realism only seem to have been sought. These are often of great beauty, and when well made are prized by collectors. Such are (#66, 134). They are not always as good to live with as more conventional ones, although nothing is known more technically superb than the so-called American 'Aubusson' clipped and modeled hooked rug. Some of these have pale flowers and leaves of a general dark tone on an ivory field (#75).

Among large and small rugs which combine realistic flowers with conventional forms, a beautiful design from the Burnham collection is (#61). The tones of such rugs are indescribable. Age has undoubtedly done wonders for them in softening and blending the tones harmoniously, giving them almost an atmosphere.

Animal forms are so varied that this class of rug can only be listed as containing some animal alone or in combination with flowers, landscape or foliage, etc. Several are here given (#53, 116, 122), and were also popular in the days of Victoria rather than earlier.

Nile green field, large blue leaves, outlined in gray, brown vase, yellow and red small flowers, black, brown and gray stems. [#90]

Probably suggested by the red amaryllis lily. Yellow, green and tan streaks in leaves, ivory field. [#91]

NOVA SCOTIAN RUGS

RARE STEPPED CRUCIFORM MEDALLION HOOKED CARPET
AMERICAN CIRCA 1800

Compact hooking. Deep tan field occupied by stepped medallion banded in blues, pink, tan and black displaying loose bouquet of lovely pink roses. The medallion bordered by pairs of cornucopias of similar roses. Finished with an unique chevroned border similarly banded to medallion. A most rare and exquisite type of hooked carpet made in Vermont. *Size: 7 feet 11 inches x 7 feet 2 inches.* [#92]

DINING–ROOM HOOKED RUG

With early trestle table. [#93]

Landscape alone is rarely seen in hooked rug design, but architectural designs especially of old homesteads and historic mansions or towns are more numerous (#144).

The hooked rug (#143) of a landscape is one obtained by R. W. Burnham in 1909 and was made by Mrs. Benjamin Franklin Wheeler who was born in the old Burnham house in Ipswich. The scene shows the old Rockport, Mass. depot made from granite blocks from the quarry of Cape Ann. It was made in 1866, exhibited at the Massachusetts Mechanics Charitable Association and awarded a diploma in 1867. Size 4′ x 6′ 6″. Mrs. Wheeler was an adept rug maker, designing her own patterns and obtaining dyeing material from mosses, barks and roots on or about the ledges of Pigeon Cove, Rockport. The rug was once in the collection of James Fenimore Cooper of Albany, N. Y.

The large oval rug (#61), from the Burnham collection, with light uncurling fronds mingled with flowers is very fine in texture, pattern, composition and color. It seems to need a more emphatic line or band of purely conventional or geometrical character between the dark border and the lighter oval of the center, but it is so beautiful that only an experienced rug designer could hope to really improve on it by any change whatsoever. It is well to compare this with Mr. John C. Spring's rug (#29). Then the above criticism has more force.

Patriotic and symbolic designs are very rare and not often well done but some, such as the American Eagle on a shield with a scroll and flower border and distant peaks in the background of the field, which is one of the best known and most remarkable of the Lawrence sale in New York, May 1921, and another which Mrs. Alice Van Leer Carrick gives in ' Antiques,' magazine (#92) and was in the Shoemaker Sale, June 1920, are excellent. The border of the latter is perhaps derived from the Chinese fence of early Anglo-American China. (#108) is probably nearly of the same date, or a little later.

Courtesy of "Antiques Magazine"

HOOKED BED COVER

Showing loops. [#94]

If one is to try to determine which of all the occurring motives in hooked rugs are the best, it could be safely said that abstract or geometric forms combined with conventionalized flowers and colors on a field in which varying tones follow the outlines of the patterns, as in old mosaics, produce on the whole the most beautiful designs.

For beginners the geometric unit or motive repeated to make a pattern is a safe one and can be made very beautiful even where part of the pattern unit is filled with 'hit-or-miss' stripes in constantly changing colors. A set pattern of four strangely drawn, finely colored roses, buds and leaves breaking into each corner of a rug with a brown inner border line and an old ivory toned field, where the center showed several of the same but differently posed flowers, was one of the most easily designed and made rugs of a New York sale at the Anderson Galleries, yet it was one of the most beautiful.

A partial list of names applied to hooked rug design would run as follows:

Hit-or-miss (from practical utilization of odds and ends) (#32).

Agate, a wavy variation of the above (#47).

Inch Square. Often made in blocks.

The Centennial, so called from a rug which took a prize at the Philadelphia Centennial Exposition 1876.

Box (#35).

Basket Weave (#32).

Wave (as in ancient glass) (#31).

Zig-Zag (savage ornament) (#40).

Log Cabin or Lincoln Log Cabin (#35).

Shell or Oyster Shell (fish scale or classic imbrication) (#36).

Lamb's Tongue, a form of the shell.

Jim Crow (#115).

Lattice or Trellis or Log, Canadian usually.

HOOKED BED COVER (1763)

Made by Mary West for self and husband Nathan.   Unclipped wool on wool basis.   [#95]

A genuine antique specimen, showing the simplicity favored by many of the
New England workers. Wool closely hooked and sheared. [#96]

A splendid example of the elaborate designs which sometimes found their way into the
best types of hooked rugs. [#97]

IMPORTANT HOOKED RUG FROM NOVA SCOTIA

Large central medallion with a group of four large red roses in the centre surrounded by spiral scrolls of leaf motifs alternating with red star flowers; tan ground. The field itself pale mulberry-red with scalloped blackish-blue edge and decorated with acanthus leaf motifs, tan and pale yellow in the centre of each side, particolored green and red in the four corners. [#98]

Size: 9 feet 5 inches x 8 feet 10 inches.

Scroll (#81) having its origin in Scandinavian Scots wood carving patterns.

Interlace, many forms and old.

Greek Wave, classic.

Persian (from rugs or decoration).

Basket of Flowers (probably from the French) (#25).

Fruit and Flowers (#79).

Harvest ears of corn, etc.

Roman Key.

Swastika.

Tile (many forms) (#37, 38, 39, 42, 43).

Sign of Fertility (from Japanese art).

Boston Sidewalk (Discs or bricks set in lines on different field).

Sun and Shadow. Exact description not known by writer.

Good Luck Chain. A border to a floral rug (#102).

Marriage or Courting Rug showing hearts and often with hearts or initials.

So many designs have an oriental quality that it is evident that the East furnished frequent inspiration.

During our Colonial period and just before and after the Revolution certain coverlets and hangings and floor coverings were produced which, although not always classifiable as hooked, were possibly done at nearly the same period and the earliest hooked or pegged rugs undoubtedly influenced somewhat this industry. I have seen three or four such pieces, some are hooked and all are of great beauty both in color and pattern. The first one noted was in Ipswich, Mass., in the Burnham collection. It was a long thin runner delicately done in yarn on a light colored base and the pattern was a pale green meandering stalk in an ' S '-like twist with flowers attached, all very conventional and graceful and beautiful, done possibly by a loose kind of hooking and

Courtesy of Caswell Barrie, Esq., Oct. 15, 1924, Anderson Galleries, N. Y.

LARGE HOOKED RUG FROM NOVA SCOTIA

A central cartouche of four large roses, old rose with foliage of rust-brown, deep and pale green on olive, bordered by mauve scrolled motifs. The field of the rug covered by a profusion of red roses with foliage in the same colors as above on olive ground. The border formed by arabesque scrolls in black outlined by pale green and mulberry-red on pale yellow and purple ground. Edge of lozenges in which pale mauve and mulberry-red prevail. A very rare and unusual specimen.

Size: 9 feet 9 inches x 7 feet 11 inches. [#99]

so, very early, really ' Antique ' as classified. The next was a large carpet found under another carpet in New England. It was like the first
piece and dated 1787 I believe or after the Revolution. This also was
done like the first piece mentioned but on lighter colored cloth and its
patterns and tones recalled that one. The third was a superb bedspread
or light rug all of wool done in long stitches on a tan colored hand-
woven woolen base with again the meandering vine on each side and
flowers in pots, figures, etc., and the maker's initials on it. This was
found in Connecticut by Mr. H. E. Keyes, Editor of *Antiques* magazine, who also owned the fourth piece, a magnificent carpet or cover
done in chain stitch, the date of which is known.

The latter two pieces I think belong in the period ' *Early* ' *1800–
1850* and are strongly like the best of the early sampler work, on a
larger scale. Other pieces still (#110, 120) are interesting as showing
the gradual transition of design toward the Early and Late periods of
hooked rug making, for in them one can see the prevalent vine form,
the scroll, and the nosegay, so often noted in the early sampler, which
finally lost their vigorous character as the later period brought in the
French flower and wreath. These lapsed finally at the end of the Victorian era into more and more strange scrolls, curves, oriental patterns
(often good) discs, wheels, raised or ' modeled ' posies and animal
forms galore, often in painfully crude landscapes, and finally plunged
into the worst kind of realistic stupidity.

These earlier pieces, of which Mr. Keyes' is perhaps the finest specimen in America, gave promise of an art development which even the
superb later hooked rugs of New England did not quite fulfill, probably because these pieces were only the tradition of European influences
then still strong in America, hence were not attractive to workers who
preferred their own ideas rather than follow foreign designs either
wholly or in part.

Courtesy of "Antiques Magazine"

ACADIAN FRENCH, NOVA SCOTIA

Probably not a stamped design, but well-balanced and carefully executed. [#100]

CHAPTER VII

Rapid Development in America

WHY DID the process and the product of hooked rug making so strongly and especially appeal to the average early American farm and seashore dweller, i.e., to what chief causes may we attribute the really unusual development of the craft on the western continent? I think this is one of the most interesting questions connected with the subject. It might be answered as follows:

The very early settlers had no mats or rugs at all except those made of rushes, or of the skins of wild animals, and had little or no time or material to make them. They were limited also when supplies came from Europe, to the importation of absolutely necessary articles. Later when rugs came across the ocean in various cargoes, from European and more eastern ports, the prices were so high that the average household often could not afford them. Hence began the use of household rags and homespun yarn in rug making and as there was little of these materials available, compared with the supply in Europe where there were more mills and more private looms, the early Americans looked on their own rug making and their own rugs with greater consideration than, for instance, did the people of Scandinavian or Scotch or English manufacturing centers where rugs were more easily made and less highly prized. In America the very scarcity of materials contributed to simplicity of design and a certain excellence. Hence also the American who could make a good rug was praised for the work, and the industry assumed an importance which it never attained in Europe. Becoming locally important it drew more and more people to rug making, induced them to try all sorts of ideas and to gather patterns from all sources.

Courtesy of Mrs. E. O. Schernikow, N. Y.

Carpet. Center oval of brilliant flowers with bluish leaves and encircled by delicate leaf scrolls in brown and old red on a sand colored field. Border, intertwined scrolls and flowers. Fine and rare example. *Size: 8 feet 4 inches* x *6 feet 3 inches.* [#101]

Coincidentally with this growing interest came the development of textile industries in America and Europe, the invention of wall paper in place of wall stenciling and of oil cloth and linoleums later

[123]

The good luck chain on a familiar type of rug design. Well drawn and colored flowers on a sand field. Often reproduced in New England and Canadian Provinces. [#102]

on. The growth of our New England and Canadian shipping industries and increasing wealth brought foreign goods and especially fabrics and designs from the greatest ports of the world. All this was grist to the mill of the rug designer, who took his or her patterns from any and every source. So the American vogue of the hooked rug grew apace. Another reason why it outstripped foreign interest in the handicraft, was, I believe, due to the enterprise of Americans in the awakened life of this continent, and perhaps more than all else to a fact already alluded to, namely, the mingling of Scandinavian, Saxon, Celt, Latin and Teuton blood which went on in those days in America much as it goes on to-day, the Celt and Latin always stimulating the Teuton and the Saxon in art. Such rapid mingling hardly came to pass in European countries, nor was there such competition there between comparatively new neighbors of different blood as continued for years here.

NOVA SCOTIAN RUG

Wool. Flowers slightly in relief.
[#103]

All this art industry beginning in America before 1800, perhaps by 1750 or earlier, this searching for pattern and expressing of ideas in the resultant product of the rug, culminated apparently in the Victorian era, after which the fever gradually died down. The migrations of Canadians and New Englanders to the west had then been considerable over a number of years and with the changing of inhabitants there came cessation of their industries in the old eastern and northern places. However, they took the craft with them and we find traces of it South and West, in the rugs made there in the last fifty years or less. The mountaineers and even the negroes in the South could make them and do now, although I have not yet seen any from the latter source as striking and bizarre as one might naturally expect from their inherent love of bright color and strong contrast. There may be many such, but I fear that the process is too slow for the average Afro-American.

Thus over the continent the handicraft spread and in all the states,

Courtesy of Messrs. Flint & Kent, Buffalo, N. Y.

Pink roses and flowers and green leaves unclassified, on a tawny field. Very beautiful. [#104]

I believe, the seeker will find to-day examples of hooked rugs either made on the spot or brought in by immigration from the eastern sea-board states and maritime provinces.

Widespread practice of the art developed it as nothing else could, for art grows by practice and appreciation and even the man on the farm took pride in the work of his wife and children. He was even working at it himself at times, especially if of a seafaring turn, for sailors never were ashamed to sew, to knit, to make mats and even scrimshaws of

MOLLY LATHROP'S BEDCOVER

Said to have been made by Molly Stark wife of Gen. John Stark for the General's niece in
1773. Of yarn hooked through a wool blanket. A prehistoric Nordic Method. [#105]

ivory nor was it called effeminate or old womanish in men who often on shipboard dropped ' mat ' work to reef a topsail in a gale, or seize a harpoon to chase the whale that was to upset and annihilate the pursuers within the half hour. Many a brave sailor turned to this art of peace, made many a purely practical hooked mat for the rigging while voyaging, and at home, after mooring for life in the well-built house of his dreams, still pursued the handicraft for purely household use and adornment, as he still does.

But why did the English not carry hooked rug making finally to greater heights? Partly, I think, because of the strange lack of inspiration manifest in English art in general, in the early Victorian epoch and just before it, although we cannot call any period in art a barren one which produced such an artist as William Blake. There was not, however, the widespread inventive force in the old country that came, and that had to come, with the life in the new. Custom and convention held people back, new homes which needed rugs were not so rapidly built, also machine-made rugs soon came in and were procurable in England for less than the Colonies could buy them. Finally the Englishman is not apt to carry things as far as his American cousin and possibly cares less for color and pattern than for solid worth and durability. So probably the old ways for him were good ways and the old designs were satisfactory and changed but little.

For the above reasons I think America led in hooked rug making and still does, but I have an idea that as there are collectors of hooked rugs in England, there are also there and in the islands and Scotland to-day many unappreciated hooked rugs in good designs. Confined to cottage use chiefly, the better class of dwellings apparently did not use them, hence except for a few collectors who, I am informed, have bought them here and there, they have remained little known and less admired by people in general. It would be interesting and I think

worth while for some American collector to hunt for them, especially
in the countryside near Leeds and Manchester, Westmorland and Scotland, especially wherever there are mills from which odds and ends of
cloth have for years been obtainable. I know of specimens elsewhere
in England made by cottagers and I believe the textile districts must
have many more in use and even making. Let us hope that some one
may succeed in finding more of them, for in the search one might come
upon further history of the introduction of the handicraft from the
continent.

Courtesy of Mrs. E. O. Schernikow, N. Y.

LARGE UNSHEARED HOOKED RUG

Farm type. Strange but effective mingling of ornament especially in center motive.

[#105a]

CHAPTER VIII

Great Artistic, Economic and Intrinsic Values

THE ARTISTIC value of the better hooked rugs is found in cer·
tain qualities which have already been referred to. First there is,
in its class, no other known handmade cloth rug surface which success-
fully rivals it in *mosaic* effect, and, in knotted rugs of wool and cotton,
only the good continental European or the oriental one offers anything
approaching it. The characteristic union, however, of form, surface
and color obtained in the wavy, free but mosaic-like texture of the oldest,
close drawn, unclipped hooked rug is not obtainable in any other way.

Aside, however, from all this there is the bizarre, original, and
bold independence, the unlooked-for and unexpected freedom of idea
in many a rug which at once interests not only the student but the layman. If comparison with any other class of rugs were to be made it
would be well, as I have already suggested, to compare hooked rugs
with Scandinavian peasant rugs and with the before-mentioned Spanish rugs from the mountain villages of Las Alpuharras, because there
is often in the texture of some of those weaves a certain likeness to
hooked rugs and the patterns and colors are bold and striking, often
beautiful. There in Spain, among the very romantic surroundings of
the valleys, certain refugee Moriscos or Moors, driven from most parts
of Spain in 1609, found homes. They and their descendants wove on
small looms under conditions similar to those of the early American
colonists, the Alpuharras blankets, rugs or coverlets shown in my article

(To Left)

This rug, of exceptional weight and thickness, measuring 5 *feet* x 6 *feet,* is made of wool yarn, closely hooked. The design is carried out in rose, blue, tan and green, against a tan and cream colored background. [#106]

(Below)

In this rare medallion-pattern hooked rug, 5 *feet* x 9 *feet,* against a tan background, appear repeated medallions in gray with bouquets of flowers in faded blue, rose and mauve. Rugs of this type are most unusual. [#107]

Courtesy Elizabeth H. Rowe, Inc., and " Harper's Bazar."   *Photos. by Walter Westervelt.*

From article *" The Native American Rug "* in *" Harper's Bazar,"* N. Y., being a revision of an unpublished article by the late Mrs. Elizabeth H. Lounsbery, called *" The Acquisitive Connoisseur."*

'The Rugs of Alpuharras,' in *Antiques* magazine for March, 1922. Both are the products of dwellers in small communities and outlying farms and mountain homes. They both tell a story, their personal

Mrs. E. O. Schernikow Sale and Courtesy of Anderson Galleries, Oct. 20, 1923

EARLY AMERICAN HOOKED RUG

Brown background sprinkled with clover, center wreath of flowers in rose, pale yellow and green. Festooned border in yellow caught with large tufted rosettes in pale rose. [#108]   *Size:* 91 *inches* x 91 *inches.*

qualities appeal to us because subconsciously we feel that some interesting and ambitious human being is trying to express him or herself in every design — good or bad. The wool (not cloth, but often yarn, and sometimes silk) in the Alpuharras rug is woven through the basic fabric of heavy linen, handmade, and is often left standing in curly loops about one quarter inch high. These Moriscos made their own yarn and the silk came from silk worms raised by them. An Irish-

Courtesy of " Antiques Magazine "

A famous pattern often used by New England rug makers of old and today. [#109]

American fabric shown in Elizabeth Calvert Hall's ' Hand Woven Coverlets,' approaches these in texture and in the effect of the higher portions. The whites in the Alpuharras rugs, however, are frequently obtained by letting the straw-white basic fabric of linen show through to make patterns. All this has been treated by the writer more in detail in *Antiques*.

In *The Arts* (magazine) November, 1921, Dr. R. M. Riefstahl, writing of Pennsylvania German pottery declares ' The return to primitive art is imminent,' adding that many now prefer rough pottery to the most subtle porcelain. Whether we do return or not, to early forms and methods, the close study and appreciation of hooked rugs to-day indicates that the rug product of the machine has lost much of the in-

Courtesy of " Antiques Magazine "

BEDCOVER, POSSIBLY HOOKED, EIGHTEENTH CENTURY

Miss Isabelle Rogers, Owner. [#110]

terest which it had, if any, for the average man of education, whether craftsman or layman.

The economic value of the hooked rug is great because its making affords an educational and improving occupation. It is a peculiarly beneficial resource not only to isolated farm dwellers but to the many

Courtesy of Caswell Barrie, Esq., Oct. 15, 1924

LARGE HOOKED RUG FROM NOVA SCOTIA

A very important specimen woven on three widths of burlap. Bold border of conventionalized foliation forming an undulated vine; moss and jade-green on olive-green edge; bunches of grapes and grapevine leaves in between. The mulberry center field is decorated with a central cartouche consisting of two groups of three large roses each, while this composition is balanced by four roses with leaves in the four corners. Fine and close hooking. Rugs of such large size can hardly be found now. [#111]   *Size: 9 feet 4 inches x 6 feet 4 inches*

who need and like such work. Especially is it helpful to those directing or pursuing occupational therapy, because of its absorbing fascination, the ease with which it can be taken up at any moment and the skill and patience it cultivates. To all of which must be added the development of the mind artistically. To manual workers, it offers a remunerative occupation of greater interest than machine work can give, one moreover which, I would repeat, can probably never be competitively commercialized. This is because the invention of a machine for making a hooked rug which would be as beautiful as the handmade article, is hardly within the bounds of possibility. This remark does not overlook the many technically fine rugs now made by machine weaving or punched by machine needle, which are still not equal to the handhooked rugs in beauty. The machine or needle-made rugs can hardly be called hooked.

Of so considerable economic value has the handicraft been deemed by the United States Bureau of Agriculture, that some years ago in a Government bulletin, now out of print, an interesting account of the industry and the location of various centers of production of hooked rugs with their promoters was given at some length. It may still be found in the best public libraries, if one is patient.

Some idea of the value of the contribution to design which the makers of hooked rugs have made may be gained by the realization that for many years inventors both abroad and in America have been trying to produce similar rug patterns by machine and with so-called improved hand implements, which are worked more rapidly than the simple farm-made hook. This has been done remarkably well by several firms in England and America but the rugs lack the character and charm of the simpler hand hooking.

Then again visitors to France in very recent years have noted that the leading French rug designers in their modern productions are

FOOKED RUG FROM NOVA SCOTIA

A design translating the gracefulness of Chippendale rocaille into the spirit of an early American interior. In the centre a cartouche formed by mulberry acanthus scrolls and spirals showing a group of roses in old rose and mulberry-red on olive-green. This cartouche is surrounded by large rose flowers of the same design and coloring. The corners are filled with arabesque stems and spiral scrolls, dark blue outlined by light blue and mulberry-red on olive-green. The edges formed by a very unusual lozenge design, mulberry and pale purple. [#112]

Size: 11 feet 8 inches x 7 feet.

either influenced by hooked rug patterns or are following the path blazed by our Colonial rug makers, in going now to the same sources of inspiration. At the Paris Salon of two years ago the similarity in design of the latest French rugs to American hooked rugs struck the writer very forcibly. Some came from private ateliers, some from commercial ones, and many were beautiful. A rug in Paul Poiret's apartment representing conventional mountains in the border and sky and stars in the middle field shows Chinese influence but has decidedly the quality of a hooked rug pattern, and Paul Poiret studies the world markets for suggestion. He knows well the source of most ornament and, I believe, even whence came the suggestion of most hooked rug patterns.

As to the intrinsic values of both old and modern rugs, it is difficult to give a just and comprehensive estimate. Mere age, or pattern, or coloring alone does not fix the value of an antique. Generally speaking, the best of the old rugs bring higher prices than any others, and no one can exactly appraise antiques. Sometimes, as in the oriental rug, age has given them an indescribable beauty of tone, although at other times, color or pattern alone or the two in combination make them very valuable. Often, however, they are practically of no value at all, even when old (except possibly as object lessons in the process of making), merely things to avoid in design, yet the writer has seen few old ones, even the ragged specimens, that were without interest of some sort, as well as many that excelled the best machine weavings and rivaled the handmade rugs of the orient. I recall one very fine rug of abstract design which I saw in a large collection. The background was a Chinese yellow with small bird and flowerlike figures of dark blue and other tones making a border. It had a strong oriental character, yet was from northeastern America, and its value to a designer or collector was great, but it was not characteristically a farm rug design, al-

Size: 12 *feet* 6 *inches* x 12 *feet* 6 *inches.* [#113]

Two large square rugs of excellent design. [#113a]

So closely and evenly hooked as to make the rug like very heavy sail canvas, bending only slightly, field beautiful ivory, brown outlines, green shaded leaves. Nova Scotian [#114]

"Jim Crow" design of a leaf pattern turned in different directions. The field shades from grey to brown and black, the leaf form is of orange, brown, purple, pink, red, green, grey blue, tan, etc., with a white outline and black and brown veins. Yet all are harmonious. Nova Scotian. [#115]
4 feet 6 inches x *13 feet 6 inches*

Collection of Mr. and Mrs. W. W. Kent

Courtesy of R. W. Burnham, Esq.

PROBABLY MADE IN NEW HAMPSHIRE   [#116]

though logically and artistically correct and beautiful, and pointed to even greater possibilities in similar design.

A hooked rug of a large size about 8′ x 12′ sold in New York in 1921 for $975.00, which gives only a faint idea of present high rug values, and at the May 1921 sale of the Lawrence Collection of Hooked rugs, at the American Art Galleries, some rugs brought over twenty-five dollars a square foot, and from this upward and down also to less than a third of this, but no one should be overinspired by these very exceptional prices, because few such rugs are found in any but the most carefully made collections formed by men of keen observation and experience.

Thus it will be seen that they must be judged from many points of view, pattern, coloring, composition, shading, age, rarity, fineness of hooking, quality of material, strength of basic fabric and condition at time of sale. It is safe to say that the average, acceptable good modern hooked rugs are worth all the way from thirty-five cents to six dollars a square foot, the limit being impossible to fix, as in other art objects of such great range in design. Five years ago I knew of two small clipped wool rugs of very fine make that were held at $500.00 but I saw no one buy them. They may have taken years to make, and are surely worth much more to-day.

The age of these rugs can of course be determined somewhat by pattern but better by tone and structure, the use of a hand-woven basic fabric of cotton or linen usually indicating an early rug, and vegetable dyes often pointing in the same direction in one of any considerable age. Vegetable dyes, however, let me say here, certainly do fade occasionally, and some colors fade more than others. Some quite old rugs look remarkably new on account of the care which has been taken in their use, but like old tapestries, beautiful specimens have often been found by collectors, dirty and discarded in stables. Some were even made from discarded horse blankets, to which fact their aroma still testified when found, and these (after cleaning), are not by any means the least valuable either in pattern, color, or fineness. The writer once found a bale of rugs in a New Brunswick barn loft, dusty and smelling of the stable, thrown out as of little value, but some were quite good and none worthless, while on the floor of the deserted farmhouse lay one or two old rugs of basket-weave pattern, left behind by the owners as no longer of any use or interest.

Courtesy of Jas. M. Shoemaker Co., N. Y.

"GOOD LUCK" HOOKED RUG, EARLY AMERICAN

Rare close hooking. Ivory field occupied at right with tan horseshoe scrolled with roses, "Good Luck" in wine-red below shoe. Mottled old-yellow borders.
Size: 4 feet 6 inches x 2 feet 10 inches. [#116a]

CHAPTER IX

A Hunt for Rugs in Canada

THE HUNTING of the rug is going on daily. Literally thousands of attics and farmhouses have been searched each year in New England and Canada and the supply in many places has given out. Nova Scotia, New Brunswick, Prince Edward Island and even Labrador have sold most of their early ones. This means increase in the value of the best old ones.

To see just how many could be found in a day, for his own collection, the writer once took a trip into almost unknown Canadian territory as far as modern rug hunting is concerned, upon the information given by a friend in Maine. The journey was begun at five-thirty A.M. and lasted until dark. It covered only one hundred miles in a motor car, traversing some of the finest forests and most inspiring table-lands of one of the Canadian provinces. Wild animals darted across the road, in the early mists, the smell of balsam, spruce and white pine was everywhere. Before noon we inquired along the way for rugs and rug makers and even the postmaster helped to direct us.

The farmhouses were few but neat, yet in them were found many worn rugs which the makers were glad to sell and nowhere was a scowl or a discourteous word encountered. One of the great rivers of North America was finally reached, wandering like the Loire of France through a beautiful wide valley, whose hillsides, looking across this broad salmon river, were distant from slope to slope three or four

Rose and mauve flowers and green leaves. Rabbits in gray and ivory. This rug was sold for $510 at Anderson Galleries Sale for Mrs. Schernikow in 1927. [#117]

Size: 50 inches x 84 *inches*

Collection of W. W. Kent

Rug made in Maine and found in Forest City, N. B. This is what the ancient Tudor scrolls from Great Britain finally became. The peacock has pink legs and seems puzzled. [#118]

miles. At last we crossed it and reached Upper Caverhill which with Lower Caverhill lay on a breezy plain that seemed to be the top of the world. At the second farmhouse, a woman answered so politely our

Courtesy of Mrs. E. O. Schernikow, N. Y.

EARLY AMERICAN HOOKED RUG

Blue and rose peacock on ivory field surrounded by leaf and fruit motifs in greens, ivory, yellow and dark brown. [#119]   *Size: 48 inches x 44 inches.*

inquiry as to rugs, that we accepted her invitation to rest a moment although she assured us she had no rugs which she could sell. In her neat and attractive sitting room we met her aged mother and enjoyed a half hour's talk with these two delightful, refined and handsome

Courtesy of " Antiques Magazine "

Signed M. F. -830. [#120]

Size: 52½ inches x 26 inches.

Scotch women, the descendants of a pioneer Scotch General, who settled the village in 17—. His Toledo sword was brought out for our inspection and also a fine old flintlock gun. Here, far from the American restlessness of modern life, almost out of the modern world but of it, as far as education and observation count, old-world breeding was kept alive, and such was the courtesy of the first who had welcomed us, that not liking to see us go back empty-handed, she wished to present me with a rug for my wife. It was an old specimen worn and almost discarded but one which I admired. It was of the basket-weave, block pattern, and 'hit or miss' in color, but harmonious. Of course, I could not accept it as a present, although she said it was of no value, so after many protests on her part, I finally induced her to accept money for it, she making the condition that the amount would be given to the fund for Church Missions, to which we agreed in a happy conclusion. She directed us to a road on our long homeward way which led by a great wayside spring bubbling out from a pipe into a hogshead, and finally we passed a number of gray-shingled homes. In one of these after a most entertaining visit, we arranged to take dinner and bought and brought away a roll of old rugs, in which we also wrapped delightful memories of the kindness, keen sense of humor, and courtesy of Miss M—— and her big brother who together ran this farm. She made many of her own rug designs excellent in pattern and color, and if she follows my advice, will never buy another design until the Canadian shop designs show improvement. Of our good designs across the border she of course knew nothing.

By this time the back of the motor was full of rugs, thirteen or fourteen, and slightly groaning, and we were glad to recross the great river nearer home than our first crossing, on a huge and primitive ferryboat, which was attached to a wheel running on a taut wire cable stretched from shore to shore. Most picturesque was the road down to

Owned by Mrs. J. Insley Blair.   Courtesy of " Antiques Magazine "

EMBROIDERED RUG

Late eighteenth or early nineteenth century.   Maine.   In   colored wools on a linen ground in various stitches.   [#121]

this barge and decidedly difficult, but we went down it by tying a drag log on one side of the motor axle, and dragging it down the slope by slow but effective jerks, to which the roll of rugs in the car added no little force and thrill.

The ferryman's shanty was very perilously hanging to the hill above the rock-strewn shore, and the barn-floor-like boat and its appurtenances were all a welcome sight; but where was the ferryman? After half an hour he appeared, coming leisurely down the bank across the river and reached us in a most remarkable small, cranky skiff rowed by an interested relative, who had encouraged our waiting by shouting well-timed guesses as to when we could start. The ferryman wore a broad and high peaked straw hat of earlier days, and his strong, bronzed face would have won a sculptor with its fine planes and perfect placidity, indeed except for its geniality it might have belonged to Charon, as he saluted us with rare dignity.

Soon we were off. Our pilot wound up the slack wire on the boat wheel, the current rushed against the side and with a resultant gentle lunge the immense craft forged ahead slowly across the mile of waters, controlled by the little wheel held by wire, and running along the taut cable, below which we traveled. We remarked that the stream was beautiful and might contain fish. ' Yes,' said the ferryman, ' they get lots of salmon here in the spring. Professor Peters got one weighed thirty pounds. They get lots of 'em,' and he seized the huge twenty-five-foot oar and began the accustomed operation of helping our speed by sculling on a primitive rest made of a tree crotch set at the stern. It was indeed all primitive, the ferryboat which seemed over one hundred years old; the huge oar; the more than six-foot man, his prehistoric face and hat, all in action now to take a small car, two men and a roll of hooked rugs across this broad and impressive waterway, and it was with a sense of great obligation and some hesitation that, as our

[150]

House and garden, with a small girl and a dog among flowers and trees. Well balanced, poorly drawn. [#122].   *Size: 5 feet 6 inches x 2 feet.*

EARLY AMERICAN

Exceptionally heavy hooking. Mosaic tan field, occupied by two circular medallions of gray and deep blue displaying standing figures of chickens. Very interesting deep multicolored chevroned border. [#123]
Size: 5 feet 8 inches x 3 feet 3 inches.

Primitively drawn animals in interesting ornament.   [#124]

A type often reproduced in hooked rugs and probably from a pattern book of circa 1890.   [#125]

craft grated on the pebbles of the further shore, we asked how much we owed. The oarsman looked at the car, then at us, and perhaps reckoned in the twenty minutes crossing, which seem like a half-hour, and finally said laconically ' Twenty-five cents.' As the motor plunged protestingly up the river-bank road, we wondered how he came to choose such an occupation and why he pursued it.

Perhaps in such an uneventful, peaceful country they can make hooked rugs best, for there, surely, the people have time to design and to execute, and do not expect or receive large pecuniary rewards. Great perhaps are their other compensations, small are their actual needs. Patience and equanimity are certainly factors in making good hooked rugs and there they have both.

We now had rugs, none ancient, but all would be improved by professional cleansing. How could they be taken best across the border, how packed and shipped? Jim solved this by getting a clean potato sack and tying them up in a sausage roll in the next town whence the Canadian Pacific took them to the customhouse at V. The trip was worth the effort and I think Jim Davis enjoyed it as much as his passenger, in spite of a balky motor.

It would be hard to analyze and describe the charm of such an experience. Other lands are more beautiful than Canada in scenery and certainly in architecture, but how seldom can a traveler freely enter the homes of natives, talk with them and learn their point of view on certain things as we did. The remoteness of the farmhouses, the evident contentment of the people of Scotch, Irish and English blood who live in them through wet autumns, severe winters and cold spring months with few outside diversions, their simplicity, their directness and above all their kind hospitality to strangers, cast a spell over the chance comer which undoubtedly adds to his appreciation of the evergreen forests, gleaming silver lakes and swift rivers that lie in sight of

The rug and the cream both hooked. [#126]

Courtesy of "Antiques Magazine"
Someone's "personality" expressed a lion, evidently farm made. [#127]

the winding gravelly roads, leading up, down and across the countryside. Then too there was the feeling that except for Indian life this part of the world is still much as it was before the American Revolution and before the Loyalists fled from ' The States,' in fact it presents a likeness of New England conditions in those earlier days, conditions that the mind of to-day cannot easily visualize. Perhaps such a journey is of greater interest than the object of it and a walking trip in certain parts of Canada would surely be as delightful to some men as were George Borrow's peregrinations in Spain or Wild Wales, even with the adventures and hazards that a journey afoot always brings.

Courtesy of Jas. M. Shoemaker Co., N. Y.

UNSHEARED HOOKED RUG, FARM TYPE. [#127a]

CHAPTER X

Careful Collecting, Using, Cleaning and Repairing

SUPERFLUOUS as they may seem, certain points about collecting are really worth consideration. First of all there is no one American district or source to be relied upon. Remember that you may find good rugs in many parts of America, north, east, south and west. Thirty years ago they still hid in forgotten attic chests unknown to the average citizen or villager. The humblest dwelling may shelter the best examples. Do not let dirt and wear discourage you if the rug has other good qualities. Look at the back and the hooking and, if the latter is fine, you will probably find that the basic material is good and the rug better than you thought at first sight, for a careful person made it. Especially look for the very old ones, as early specimens are frequently good in character, but be careful that they have not through careless usage become rotten. The reason for the excellence of early pieces is that our ancestors were more painstaking and enthusiastic makers than were later people.

Do not pay great prices and do not be afraid to pay decent ones for whatever you see that is good. Treat the seller as fairly as you can afford to. Collect a number of specimens and as you add to them discard from your collection the less valuable ones. Buy even of reputable city dealers who are by no means always high priced. Keep up this weeding-out process and you will gradually improve your collection and your knowledge.

Pennsylvania Dutch (?) Eagle with marine forms. Discs
like those on Pennsylvania Dutch barns. [#128]

Early American unclipped, pure wool yarn, cream field,
white swans, black and tan border. [#129]

[158]

CANADIAN UNSHEARED WOOL [#130]

AN EARLY AMERICAN RARE RACING RUG

Probably made for a winning jockey and possibly Canadian.
Exceptionally fine fluctuating tan field, displaying a jockey
cap in red and ivory before two crops, within a dainty
wreath of pink roses. Curious ring corners. [#131]

Size: 3 feet 7 inches x 2 feet 1 inch.

[159]

Do not buy odd or bizarre patterns unless there is an undefinable quality of excellence or of primitive vigor in them, or unless some other good reason appeals strongly to you. If you are sure, buy at once and carry off your find, or you will regret the loss of a good example. Sometimes it pays to buy a bale to get a single splendid piece.

MASONIC RUG

Possibly made for an architect. Modern. [#132]

You will find rugs in the hands of peddlers, book and other agents and on floors, under carpets even, also stored away in forgotten nooks and sometimes even hung for days on the back fence. Look for them on sofas, chair seats and footstools, and ask about them. If you talk to farm dwellers anywhere and everywhere in America you will find hooked rugs where you least expect to see them. In a quiet corner of Canada they once gave prizes, in at least one district school I know of, for the best rug design made by a scholar and this was many years ago, so the grown-up scholar says to-day.

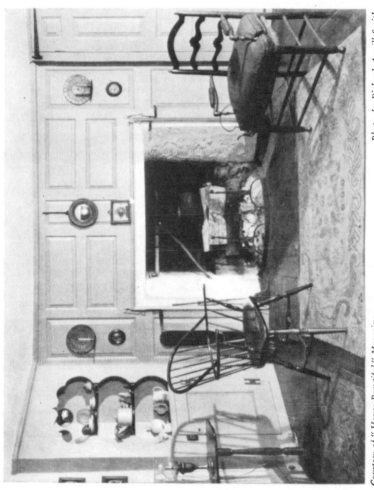

Photo. by Richard Averill Smith.

THE OLD DUTCH LIVING ROOM AT MILL FARM [#133]

Home of Mr. and Mrs. Edward C. Gude, Harrison, N. Y., in which French Provincial and Windsor arm chairs and very beautiful New England hooked rugs harmonize. Mill Farm is the site of an ancient camping ground of the Indians where each year, it is said, they met, hoping to see in the mist of the falls, the form of a deer foretelling a good harvest.

Besides the pleasure of collecting these rugs for their own beauty, about which few collectors wish or really need much instruction, there is a word or two to say as to the proper places in which to use them, either in collections or in household use.

Very few hooked rugs are appropriate for a city house throughout, unless it is of a Colonial or some very plain type, calling for furnishings of comparatively early or simple character, such as our ancestors used to build in both city and country. Such houses are not common in the city. There are a few rare types of Victorian hooked rugs in geometrical and even in floral patterns which harmonize with other kinds of interiors as well as with those mentioned above, but such rugs are scarce and usually quite expensive, costing fully as much and often more than certain good oriental productions. The prevailing types of hooked rugs, those which can be secured by the average householder without much trouble or too great expense, are most effective when placed in those city, suburban or country houses in which there is a great freedom in furnishing, or of which the architecture is strictly of so-called Georgian, Colonial or the plainer types of English and provincial French design. Also any simple house of unpronounced character is usually suitable for them. Mrs. Carrick says, ' I sometimes wonder if people really appreciate the simple charm of " drawn-in " (hooked) rugs. Oh, I know connoisseurs do, and that, now and again, unbelievably high prices are paid for historical or landscape patterns. But I mean everybody, everybody who loves old furniture, and its unpretending homeliness which was the background of our ancestors' lives. In no sense do they become lofty chambers of magnificence; rooms where Sheraton settees in the golden tones Time has polished to a subdued radiance, or subtly carved ribbon-backed Chippendale chairs agree in eighteenth century perfection with inlaid Hepplewhite card-tables, for these demand the finest Oriental weaves. But with the plainer Colo-

Courtesy of "Antiques Magazine" and "Am. Carpet & Upholstery Journal" N.Y.

HOOKED RUG (AUBUSSON PATTERN)

Owned by New Hampshire Historical Society. Size of rug 6 *feet* 4 *inches* x 3 *feet* 4 *inches*. An extraordinarily fine specimen in both design and workmanship. While the source of hooked rug pattern is frequently a matter of doubt, there can be no question that the more elaborate examples, such as this, were inspired by Aubusson carpetings. [#134]

nial oak (if we are fortunate enough to have it) or peasant furniture from England and France; with Windsor or stenciled chairs and the drop-leaved tables and the flat-topped, unpretentious highboys that all our forefathers once possessed, they are admirable. Indeed, I don't know any other thing that quite takes their place; they have a finer color value than either braided or woven rugs, and infinitely more personality and presence.' To which I would add that French provincial or bourgeois furniture certainly goes well with them.

It is a mistake to try to place them on a floor with many of the oriental makes, for they do not often blend well. Sometimes rare patterns and faded tones in hooked rugs, especially those where the oriental influence is pronounced, will harmonize with the Eastern knotted products, but this is rarely the case. Some hooked rugs too are of such exquisite fineness, soft tones, good pattern, harmony of color and delicate construction that they are perfectly suitable for hangings and not at all serviceable as rugs. Especially is this true where age has weakened the fabric. If this is so, and they are valuable, as they probably are, then they are better lined and hung on the wall like tapestry than laid on the floor to be walked upon. Such a rug is the one at 'The Sign of the Motor Car' (#15) and others here given (#68).

When they were used as coverings on furniture as they occasionally were, only those of very closely hooked character were available, for if they were loosely hooked, the basic material was sure to show through on bends or curves. The more tightly they are hooked the better they are for the purposes of upholstery.

It is often said that they will outwear oriental knotted rugs. This statement must be taken with qualifications, and it is not true where the hooked rug is badly made, though in other cases it may be so. Much depends upon the care taken of either kind of rug. If a hooked

Courtesy of Messrs. Clifford & Lawton, N. Y.

Such a delightful room almost begs for another fine rug. [#135]

rug shows signs of pulling out, or raveling or wearing thin, it should be examined at once and carefully repaired by a competent worker. Sometimes the basic material grows flimsy or weak or even rotten with age or misuse and a stitch or loop in times saves more than nine loops. Repairs at this stage are not expensive, and much less than for oriental rugs. If a rug must be bound or lined let it be done not too tightly, so as not to draw up the rug in wrinkles at the corners, as careless repairers occasionally do.

It is better to do the regular household cleaning of them by careful sweeping on an outer porch floor, but now and then they should also be laid on the lawn grass or out on the snow and beaten both on face and back with a flexible carpet beater not too vigorously. Shaking is decidedly bad for them and not effective. *Never fold an old rug but always roll both old and new when necessary to remove or transport them.*

Whenever and wherever you buy always be sure that the rug is clean when it finally goes into your collection. It is best to send old or dirty ones directly to a reliable cleaner and repairer, not of oriental rugs but of hooked rugs. Only he can properly clean and mend them. A poor cleaner may let the colors run, in drying, or ruin them by bad repairs and poor binding. The cost of cleaning is now from five to fifteen cents a square foot. Insure them when sending away as the fire risk is often considerable. They should certainly be cleaned by an expert process, not only for decency, but to bring out the softness and the harmony of tone, almost atmospheric, which seems peculiar to good, old ones. There are places where this is well done in or near several of the larger cities. No one knows the full value of even a very dirty, ' caked ' and old hooked rug until it is cleaned. Age gives a tone which, as all rug collectors know, nothing else can supply, and if the pattern is good, the cleaning will be a surprising revelation of its tones and

A good room, good furniture, good rugs, all in keeping. [#136]

A room worthy of the fine rugs shown. One longs to know the colors. [#137]

Undoubtedly these rugs add a little color and charm to even this delightful interior. [#138].

[169]

texture. The designer who made an excellent pattern is apt to have used a fairly good color combination and age always improves the latter.

I would even go so far as to say that a bad color scheme often becomes excellent through age and dirt and wear. Therefore, have your old rugs cleaned, generally speaking, and especially when they are very old or very dirty, and then the saying cannot with truth be repeated, in your house at least, that ' the love of hooked rugs is not an acquired taste, but an acquired smell.' Much as most of us love the farm, the barnyard odors should be kept in the barnyard and some very beautiful old rugs are so odorous before cleansing as to suggest that the ancient horse blanket aforesaid really gave up its substance to their creation, whereas they come often from the shoes that pass over barnyard and floors. Odors can be entirely killed by expert cleansing.

Rugs which are of light construction or soft, light tones should never be placed where they will receive too great or constant wear. Better keep them for less frequented places, putting tough and new ones at doorways and hearths and telephone stands. New rugs are really improved by wear and even by dirt, and so even the Asiatics believe, for they lay their newer knotted rugs on the soil, in the streets and out in the sun and even drive sheep over them, to say nothing of less honest methods of washing in chemicals and fading by devices, which are not for us to use on hooked rugs, although some dealers and even householders try to ' freshen them up ' by painting on new dyes, and age them by false dates slightly altered from modern ones.

I prefer not to have old rugs bound. Where possible, it is better to make good the old borders. Braided borders were used by early makers, but nothing is better than the strongly made hooked border, done on double burlap turned in for this purpose. However, in certain cases cloth bindings are the only thing to put on to save the rug.

A simply and well furnished dining-room with a simple, formal rug of good tone.   [#139]

CHAPTER XI

*Various Sizes, Age, Modern and Future Production and
Development*

THE SIZES of hooked rugs known to the writer vary from two feet
or less to twenty-five feet long by different widths, although the
square form of very great area is unusual. In the Lawrence Collection,
before mentioned, were some measuring over seventeen feet long.
Large rugs were actually carpets, made in separate pieces and finally
sewed together so carefully that the seams did not show distinctly, as
was often the case with Spanish and other rugs made on a small loom.
The time taken to make such large rugs must have been considerable,
but the workers were proficient and several people, often the whole
family, at a ' rug frolic ' worked at once on the different portions, as
also would have been the case with workers at a ' sewing bee.'

The commonest sizes are of the hearth rug or door mat dimen-
sions, frequently controlled by the size of burlap feed bags or potato
sacks, which were easily obtained on the farm, and coffee sacks are
sometimes used even to-day as seen in some Philadelphia collections.
Stair and hall runners are sometimes found fully twenty-two feet long.

As to the age, many connoisseurs do not believe that even the oldest
American rugs were made much over one hundred years ago. One
well-known collector owns a rug which, from reliable information, was
made close to 1820. The writer, as before stated, now believes that
hooked rugs of closely similar fabrics were *commonly* made in Eng-

[172]

A small and formal room needs two conventional or formal rugs, but certain geometrical patterns would also be in keeping. [#140]

[173]

land and Scotland fully one hundred and fifty years ago and you have seen that Miss Macbeth credits the process with an age of four hundred years, and Miss Haslund states that the Bronze Age knew it. The catalogue of the Lawrence Collection sale, states that 'the hooked rug' *originated* in America during the Colonial days of the early eighteenth century, but while this date may be correct for their first making in America, yet in view of all these later researches here given, they are, I am firmly convinced, of very much older foreign origin, although certain ways of hooking may be peculiar to this country. Lately it has been said that they are peculiarly Victorian, but while very many were made from 1850 to 1890, many now known were made long before and thousands of quite old ones must have been destroyed in America.

The late Hamilton Easter Field who owned an interesting collection and had studied them for years writes, 'Their age has been greatly exaggerated, and I doubt if the oldest rug in my collection was made over one hundred years ago.' This too *may* be true as to his American rugs.

Those Americans who made the early rugs, as a rule appreciated them greatly, for the work both of design and execution is considerable and the results often commanded the admiration and praise of visitors and friends as they do to-day. Mr. Burnham relates that 'an old lady in Ipswich, Mass., told me that when she was a girl, " Mother always kept the hooked rugs bottom side upwards. When company was expected, Mother would sit by the front window, watching for them; and as soon as they hove in sight, she would say, ' Sally, turn the rugs, while I mind the door.' " '

For many years, perhaps from 1900 to 1910 little interest was shown in them by the general public. They had been, even on the farms, often relegated to kitchens, stables and attics. Many people never had seen or known of them. Twenty or more years ago they

Courtesy of Messrs. Clifford & Lawton, N. Y.

A " good luck chain " rug and a big conventional primitive floral rug, such as these suit admirably any room of this type provided that the carpet is darker and harmonious. [#141]

The low-posted "spool" bed, as small, with the ramp bed and print-covered chairs [#142]

[176]

were arousing a little interest among a few people, and several years before the Great War, many good collections were made by connoisseurs and dealers in New England. I saw some excellent ones in Boston then, at Mr. E. C. Howe's shop on Boylston Street and was struck with their great value artistically, as well as with the prices asked. These prices have been proved reasonable by present commercial values.

View of Rockport, Maine. Hooked and clipped by Mrs. B. F. Coburn. Once in collection of J. Fenimore Cooper, Esq., Albany, N. Y. Now in Langhorne collection, Richmond, Virginia. [#143]

It goes without saying, that there is no more charming, appropriate and durable floor covering for the town or country houses of our Early American revival than the hooked rug, but some, like the best oriental weavings are of such fineness and general excellence that they are more properly placed in museums for study than used as floor rugs.

There is, however, no art museum, known to the writer, which owns a full and good collection, but doubtless there will be such collections before many years, from which student and designer may learn

to appreciate the beautiful qualities and the wide range of possibility
in their design. The Metropolitan Museum of New York and others
have tardily begun to collect them.

Nowadays there are many centers of production. Mr. Warren
Weston Creamer of Waldeboro, Maine, says that " Waldeboro has long
been noted for its very fine rugs. Between the years 1860 and 1885 there
were a great many artistic rugs made in this section. The colorings

Courtesy of R. W. Burnham, Esq., Ipswich, Mass.

Early American. Unsheared. Remarkable mosaic effect of closely set loops. [#144]

were beautiful and during that period the work was splendidly done.
I think the best were made between 1875 and 1885 reaching the highest
point of perfection at approximately the latter date. Since that time
the quality of the work has slowly retrograded and the quantity of rugs
produced has diminished until at present there is practically no hooking done here and the few that are made are very poor as to quality and
design. Beautiful rugs were made much earlier and I have had a great
many that were probably produced as early as 1830. These were usu-

[178]

ally of yarn, very soft in texture and on a homespun linen foundation. There were also a good many of the needlework or reed stitch type of rugs made approximately one hundred years ago. These are becoming very scarce."

From this and other data it is plain that the craft has been intermittently pursued there as in other places. Mr. and Mrs. Douglas Volk were among the earliest admirers and makers of a knotted rug (I believe). Mrs. Albee's 'Abnakee' hooked rugs were made at Pequaket, N. H., for many years, and she says that Mr. Volk's appreciation inspired her. In Maine, besides individual work by the farm people and local or visiting artists, there was recently an established industry at Cranberry Island, Maine. In Crawfordsville, Indiana, the 'Ouia' rug industry was begun by Mrs. Mary McM. Kingery before 1906, inspired by Mrs. Albee's work. The United States Department of Labor Bulletin, November 1904, in 'Revival of Handicrafts in America' gives several addresses of rug making centers, i.e. Miss F. L. Goodrich, Allenstand, Madison County, North Carolina; Mr. and Mrs. T. L. Bayne, Russellville, Tennessee; and others. Some of these industries are now abandoned or have changed hands. Mrs. John Titcomb, of Connecticut, makes excellent ones and has organized her workers in a New England village. At Troy, N. Y., there is a firm which makes hooked rugs for the modern rug demand, a technically excellent hooked rug is now made at Auburn, Me., by machinery. The Hearthstone Studios of Mrs. A. M. L. Phillips, New York City, supply hooked rugs made to order in country homes, as well as Early American pieces, and Mr. A. P. Porter, Glen Head, L. I., N. Y. makes very fine ones called 'Percellen.' In most of our large cities and in Montreal and other Canadian cities, there are places where various sorts of weaving are carried on, and hooked and other rugs made and sold, such as the Bucilla rug at R. H. Macy & Co.'s, often in the local Women's Exchanges. In Boston there are very many sale places, and the South End and other missions make rugs. There is hardly an ' antique ' store worthy of the name in the large cities that does not carry old hooked rugs and many also sell the modern ones. In Ipswich, Mass., Mr. R. W. Burnham's industry collects, cleans, and repairs hooked rugs especially, and especially well, and many skillful women are employed. Mr. Burnham has a standing offer of a reward for exact information as to when and where the first hooked rugs were made in America and in many ways is encouraging their manufacture such as supplying patterns and frames and hooks, etc. In fact, there is no source from which more can be learned in object lessons on the general questions of hooked rug making, qualities, repairs, care, cleaning, etc., than from his workshops.

Some of the leading stores in the larger cities to-day are making collections of rugs not only for immediate sale but because they foresee that in a few years there will be an insatiable demand for the finest early specimens of the American ones.

To prophesy is easy. To-day it seems as if the value of the best examples of Early American hooked rugs would steadily increase as the years pass, for the vogue steadily spreads further and further afield.

As to the future of modern hooked rug making, the outlook is promising. If the present interest does continue to grow, not only among skilled designers, but on the farms, we shall surely see results that will rival, if not surpass what was done in the nineteenth century. There is, as the writer has found, a steadily growing interest in the production of these rugs to-day in the New England and Canadian farming districts and several people are interested in supplying good designs to take the place of the formerly bad, ' ready-stamped ' ones.

CHAPTER XII

Scotch Rugs

THE following letter corroborates Miss Ann Macbeth's earlier discoveries and gives an interesting account of Scottish rug hooking;

CRAIGIE HALL
CRAMOND BRIDGE
WEST LOTHIAN

29th April, 1930

W. W. KENT ESQ.,
   28, Valley Road,
     Bronxville,
      New York.

DEAR SIR,

With regard now to your letter of March 27th about the making of " Hooked Rugs " in this country, this, of course, has been a home or a fireside craft for many generations but I am afraid we do not take sufficient cognizance of these things to collect specimens or write up their history as you do in America. After receiving your letter, I got one of our Artists to make a little excursion in the neighbourhood here and to a district where these rugs are still being made, and I enclose copy of notes he made, along with five photographs of the actual rugs which he got.

This district referred to — Coburnspath — is on the East coast of Scotland, not very far from Edinburgh, and if you are ever in this country, it would interest you probably to pay a visit to the district. There are some interesting old castle remains and old world things that you would no doubt like to see.

There are of course a good many rugs of the Hooked kind in Westmoreland and in different parts of England, chiefly in the South. I may have an opportunity of getting photographs or some detailed information of them in the near future and if I find them of sufficient interest shall let you know. . . .

Yours faithfully,
JAMES MORTON

Hooked Rugs

Notes taken during a visit to COBURNSPATH on April 10th, 1930

Coburnspath, in Haddingtonshire, is a typical Scottish Fishing village which has retained its traditions in crafts-work and speech. *Norwegian* influences are still in evidence as shown by words such as *skir* still used.

The rock formation on this part of the coast is of the Calciferous series, a soft sandstone which is very easily cut.

The approach to the Harbour is a long tunnel cut through the rock and at Coburnspath and in the vicinity are several smugglers caves fashioned in the cliffs. One of these, still known as the Brandy Cave is mentioned in the Heart of Midlothian (Scott). Later these caves were used as store-rooms for legitimate trade. The size of one of these is such as to provide accommodation for ship loads of a then flourishing trade.

The Hooked Rugs in this district are used almost exclusively for floor coverings and each cottage has an ample supply of hand-made rugs in a variety of weave.

Type 1 of Scottish Rug from Coburnspath. [#149]

Type 1A of Scottish Rug. [#150]

Type 2 of Scottish Rug. [#151]

There seems to be no history attached to these rugs, nor, when old, any value. The older inhabitants say they were made in the same way, as long ago as they can remember and that at all times the canvas upon which the rugs were worked was purchased with the design marked thereon.

Several distinct types are made but in each case the material used is furnished from old used clothes and other rags.

The Making

Type 1 & 1A

Jute canvas is stretched on a frame and rags torn into strips are pulled through the canvas so as to make a loop about three quarters of an inch high on the face. The cloth is pulled tight on the back and the wedging of the cloth through the jute prevents the loops from slipping. The loops are either cut or left standing. (#149, 150)

When the whole area of the rug is covered with loops, a thick paste — made of flour and boiling water — is smeared over the reverse. It is said that a rug lasts longer so treated. This process is called battering. A covering of canvas is sewed on the back to complete the rug.

Type 2 & 2A

This type is made from unravelled woollen garments, such as stockings, jerseys, etc.

They are hooked in the same way as type 1, but do not last so long unless the weave is very close and tight.

Type 2 shows a loose rug with only 2 or 3 strands of wool to each hooking. (#151)

Type 2A is made with 20 or 30 strands and left uncut. (#152)

Type 2A of Scottish Rug. [#152]

Type 3

This is not a Hooked rug. Balls of coloured wools are sewn on to the face of the canvas and though the effect is pleasing the rug is inclined to be limp and fails to lie well. (#153)

" Hookie Rugs "

Hartsop, Pattendale

Miss Ann Macbeth searched to discover the origin of rag rugs. Found them very general in North Ireland, Scotland, North England, Wales and in Norway.

They do not appear to be in use in the South.

An ancient tomb in Norway disclosed remnants of Hooked rugs and it is probable that the first specimens came to Scotland with the ships of the " Maid of Norway " and as Miss Macbeth says, " Being part of the unfortunate Maiden's trousseau should have been returned to her native land."

The general use to which these hooked materials were put was for bed covering and even now in some cottages in the Lake District they are so used.

As a general rule the makers are content with a serviceable article and do not bother about producing a pleasing effect. Rare exceptions however occur and Miss M. occasionally comes across some very fine specimens.

In the encouragement of Village Industries, Miss Macbeth judges at Rural Womens Institutes, etc. and is therefore familiar with these rugs made in the English Lake District. The best examples she has seen were made in Galloway and the types although varied were in general on the lines of the types described above.

Type 3 of Scottish Rug (Sewed). ⌊#153⌋

CHAPTER XIII

Possible Sources of Rug Design

IT HAS already been said that the rug makers went to all sorts of sources for suggestion and the following plates have seemed to illustrate this so well that they are included here.

If one wishes to learn something of the early date at which hooked rugs were made in America, it would be well to read Gertrude De Wager's excellently told tale of her Grandmother's work on them. The latter learned dye making for rug cloth from her mother in Eastham on Cape Cod in 1778. This takes rug making well back into the Eighteenth century, which is not an early date for Scotch and English makers but fairly so for American. Gertrude De Wager's article is in ' Antiques Magazine' for June 1925 and is a charming picture of the process, simply told, but so fully and well that one can visualize the older woman at this occupation which fascinated her as completely as it did her grandchild who so graphically describes it. We can almost see the girl running to her Grandmother with the bag of old woolen pieces and observe the joy of the old lady at having them. Eastham was where Prince, the first Governor of Massachusetts, made his early home and planted his famous pear tree, and the site is near the present highway bend not far from the Penniman homestead, a peaceful and beautiful location in a charming old settlement. Just the place where one might expect to find hooked rug making going on, so removed is it from the distractions and noises of modern life. No wonder that in this place it was possible to learn how to make such harmonious patterns without black outlines bordering the various details of the rug, but with tones and shades of color that even in photographs melt together and show us now how nearly the aged and enthusiastic worker equalled the effects so sought by the most inspired rug makers of Eastern Persia. If some day Americans in the United States or Canada should quite equal such work it will be attained, not by machinery, but by manual work akin to the old-time method of making the hooked rug.

BORDER PATTERNS

Showing forms akin to those used on hooked rugs and possibly
derived from oriental rugs and pattern books for embroidery
in Germany and France. [#154]

PART OF AN ENGLISH EMBROIDERED CARPET

XVIII century, worked in cross stitch and chain stitch. Note the similarity to hooked rugs
of early date. [#155]

[193]

Owned by L. Earle Rowe

OLD BLUE WARE

Such a floral border is conventionalized sufficiently to fill well the proper spaces, the blossoms well placed for emphasis and balance. Starting with these, it was natural to introduce flowers from the worker's own garden. New York from Brooklyn Heights. Designed by Tom. Guy Wall and made by Stevenson. [#156]

THE LETTER OF INTRODUCTION [#157]

THE ERRAND BOY BY SIR DAVID WILKIE

The old blue Anglo-American china, especially in border patterns, was a fertile source of suggestion, but often the designer went to the garden for color and form and possibly to the china for conventional guidance. [#158]

Courtesy of Mrs. E. O. Schernikow, N. Y.

HANDWOVEN COVERLET

Very rare and unusual old handwoven coverlet in old blue and white. Large star in centre surrounded by heavy floral wreath. American eagle at each corner of centre panel. Foot-wide border shows floral design similar to centre. Fringe on three sides. Made about 1825. Shows ornament then in vogue. [#159]   *Size: 76 inches x 62 inches*

Spode Variant of Willow Pattern

In this the fence, the central tree, the bridge decoration of perforations and the turf and border at top all invite copying by rug workers. [#160]

[197]

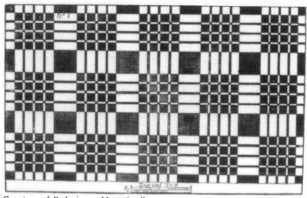

This is like the "inch square" patterns on rugs. [#161]

Akin to a Turco-Persian interlace. From "a true valentine" of
1823, owned by Mrs. C. A. Adams. [#162]

EMBROIDERY UNITS

Early XVII Century, and often found in later designs. [#163]

A VALENTINE MAZE
[#164]

OLD SPODE TRANSFER PATTERN

Showing border like hooked rug in author's collection.

BERLIN WOOL PATTERN IN GERMAN STYLE

In composition and detail much like a hooked rug pattern. [#166]

SANDWICH GLASS

The Frigate Constitution. Note the use of the hearts and stars in border, common in hooked rug design as was the elevation of a ship. [#167]

American Daguerrotype Case of the nineteenth century. Pattern of Victorian character not unlike hooked rug designs. [#168]

CHAPTER XIV

General Consideration of the Art

UNDOUBTEDLY this is the most important rug handicraft developed in the western continent, and to Americans must go the chief praise for its development even if now we must surely concede that it is not American in its origin. It is the most important rug handicraft, first because of the great beauty of its finest products, early and late; second because it developed in people who were not reached by many such helpful influences, a very considerable knowledge of design, causing them to observe and note not only facts and phases of nature, but to study the designs of earlier times; third because it afforded, both to the isolated and to those in larger communities, an avocation and diversion more engrossing than any then available; fourth because it encouraged thrift and helped entire families to greater comfort and decency; and fifth because it especially led to keen interest and pride in manual work.

This last point is one which appeals strongly to us to-day. Never has there been a time in the history of the world when absorbing handicrafts were of greater value to humanity. Our population has drifted into cities at an alarming rate and of these city dwellers a too numerous part are engaged in work in which, if we may judge by their carelessness, they plainly show a lack of interest. Miss Ann Macbeth says of machine work in Great Britain ' we have lost the holy spirit.' There are to-day in many of our crowded centers people, especially the Latins, who can conceive and execute designs of great merit for all sorts of things, yet they are forced to earn an immediate living in work which is not only uninteresting, but really harmful to mind, morals and gen-

Courtesy of W. W. Creamer, Esq., Waldeboro, Me., and American Art Association, N. Y.

PAIR OF WALDEBORO, MAINE, HOOKED RUGS

Each with a posy of scarlet, lavender, blue and white blossoms with leaves in two greens, leaf scrolls in similar colors with light center on dark field. Exhibited at the Maine Dealers Antiques Exposition, Portland, Me., 1930. [#169 and #169a]   *Each 5 feet 10 inches x 3 feet 10 inches.*

eral health. I will not enumerate here the various societies which have been formed to overcome this, and turn individual talent into the proper channels, but they are easily found in town and city.

[205]

The great manufacturing cities employ thousands at machines which kill initiative and make their operators more and more like automatons. We know how uninteresting work breeds social discontent. To travel in a rut is killing. The joy of creation is one of the most precious human attributes, and few of us realize how much the hard-worked farm dweller was rested and reinvigorated by turning to the

By courtesy of W. W. Creamer, Waldeboro, Me., and American Art Association, N. Y.

Antique piece, unusually thick, large scarlet and white blossoms and green leaves and detached flowers on soft brown ground. This was formerly in the Gen. Knox Mansion, Thomaston, Me. [#170]   *Size: 5 feet 4 inches x 2 feet 10 inches.*

work of finishing that beautiful hooked carpet of medallions and flowers to cover the floor of the 'spare room.' Into it perhaps she (and possibly he) put the reminiscence of some flower garden which they could never own, or the vision of a journey they could never take. The foreign patterns brought to mind stories of cruises told by father or son. China, India, Japan and even the islands and coasts of the seven seas laid some of their romance and delight at her tired feet when she copied the strange designs from tea chest, embroidery or ivory carving that somehow had drifted to a neighbor's closet or to the parlor ' what-not.' A fence design on a Chinese pattern plate, as already said, gave the motive, I really believe, for the border of a rug (#160) which has been valued at a great price, and where but from classical sources could the worker have derived its horns of plenty and the center, a stepped medallion?

Mankind can keep the joy of life alive if helped by such aids; can sail out of life's doldrums, if there is ever so little breeze from such a

Courtesy of W. W. Creamer, Esq., Waldeboro, Me., and American Art Association, N. Y.

Leaves in mulberry, green and soft brown on a buff field. [#171]
Size: 2 feet 8 inches x 4 feet 9 inches.

quarter, but he must have some task or diversion which inspires or at least interests and spurs him on, before he can catch the breeze. Surely the New England and Canadian hooked rug maker found a great relaxation from drudgery and a stimulation to create, in the entire process

[207]

of rug production. The results show it. Even the bad designs and poor execution in rugs indicate that some found pleasure in their work and while such poor results do not afford us pleasure, we can always hope that in the next rug made the bunch of roses and ferns did not look so painfully and falsely realistic or that the next cat and kittens ' hooked ' had more than one eye apiece and legs that were not out of joint.

But do not imagine that all early rug makers were poor draftsmen or bad and merely bizarre colorists. Far from it. Many American rugs were made by people who could compete with good foreign designers. This is certain from their finished work, now held in great esteem. There are many hooked rugs which could not have been better designed or made in the France or Italy of their day, so perfect is the composition, the conventionality, the coloring and the execution. Such work will always command the praise of critics and indicates the excellence which can still be attained by earnest and able workers, even though the designs be in a different and new vein, as indeed they should be.

If we believe that the limit of design in this handicraft has been reached, we cannot argue for its continuance; better try new fields. But it is widely believed that the possibilities in developing even the older ideas, methods and designs are so great as to warrant all the encouragement that we can give to the modern workers. There is also a great field here for new color combinations, new patterns, new shapes. For all these the vein of suggestion is not yet exhausted, and no so-called school yet limits the range of experiment in any direction. Mrs. Albee tried American Indian designs, in her Abnakee rugs, others have done the same, and there are available all the accumulations of the Smithsonian and other museums to study. Not that I would advise pure copying. Copying is perfectly admissible, even desirable, at times and what an Indian worked into his or her rug or basket or porcupine-quill box, or drew on a deer skin or even on the sand, will often bear our translation into rug language. Especially when using Indian sym-

Courtesy of W. W. Creamer Esq., Waldeboro, Me., and American Art Association, N. Y.

HOOKED CARPET

Light field, oval medallion of baskets and bouquets of roses and other flowers and leaves in deep colors with border of flower baskets and lavender ribbon ties. C-scroll border in two shades of cobalt. Bound. [#172]

Size: 11 feet 7 inches x 8 feet 8 inches.

bols and forms should the designer strive to create harmonious backgrounds and borders, or contrasting and effective features.

That the art of the American Indian (or Amerind art) has already influenced hooked rug design somewhat, is a proof that designers before now have realized its adaptability to hooked rug patterns. How-

ever, I do not believe that Americans will do the best work by following too closely any one phase or school, but they certainly can, by
studying well what has preceded, and by learning to design appropri-
ately for the hooking process, insure its greatest development.

It would be no small accomplishment for America not only to
have preserved the art, but to improve it for future generations. Some
people do not believe that moderns can be making hooked rugs equal-
ing in quality those made by early workers. Such critics believe that
there is an indefinable something lacking in all the modern work that
they have seen; that the knowledge of design, drawing and color taught
by school or observation rather hampers than helps, or else that the
simple life of the early colonists lent such a hand to the craftsman, as
modern life cannot offer; that modern designs are too clever, too knowing, too correct and not expressive of personality; that the ancient vigor
is no longer apparent.

All this I cannot agree with. We have lost much in purity of design by the passing of the early Colonial life, but not everything, and
we must not forget that time and wear did much to make early hooked
rugs beautiful for later generations. Therefore time and wear will
again help to beautify designs of the present day, for the future, and I
have seen a new hooked rug of large size, based on the careful study of
design, color and technique of an early piece, which although a modern
product held its own, even while new, with some of the very best early
American examples. Also several small modern rugs came to my
notice recently which compared favorably with the old work and one
in particular was a work of the highest order both in color and pattern.
Therefore I hold with many others that hooked rug making in America
has never died, but is full of life and promise. May it prove so.